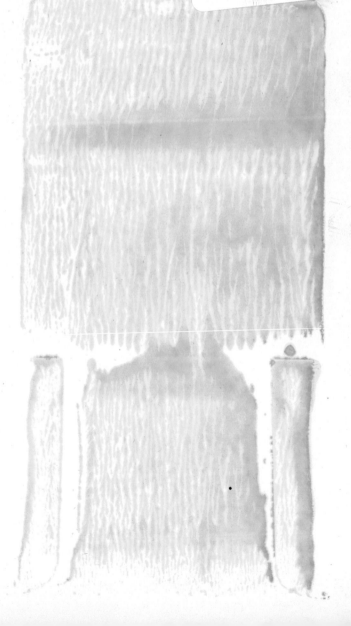

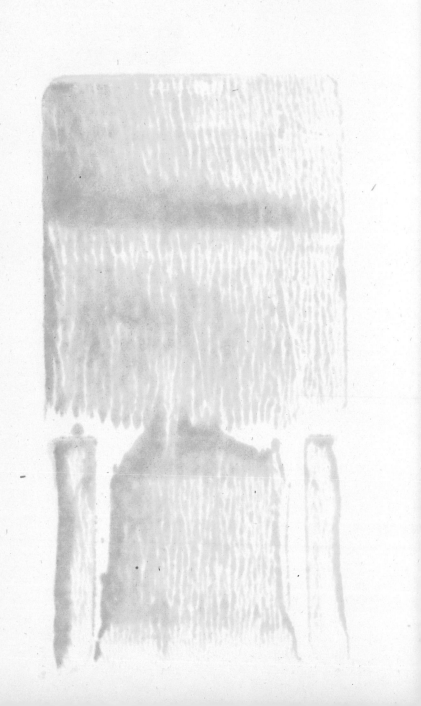

Oliver Cromwell

1 CROMWELL
From the portrait by Samuel Cooper

2 CROMWELL'S SIGNATURE AS PROTECTOR, 1657

Oliver Cromwell

and his Times

PETER YOUNG

*'None climbs so high as he
who knows not whither he is going'*

ARCO PUBLISHING COMPANY, Inc.
NEW YORK

First published 1963 *in the United States by*
Arco Publishing Company, Inc.
480 Lexington Avenue, New York 17, N.Y.

Second printing, 1965

© *Peter Young, 1962*

DA
426
. Y6
1963

Printed in Great Britain

PREFACE

THE late Isaac Foot is reported as saying:

'I judge a man by only one thing. Which side would he have liked his ancestors to fight on at Marston Moor? That's all I want to know about him.'

I may as well say at the outset that my personal sympathies are with the Royalists. For this reason since, like Sir Philip Warwick, 'I have no mind to give an ill character of Cromwell', I have tried to let him tell his own story and to look at him through the eyes of his contemporaries.

Until Carlyle's great work was published in 1845 Cromwell was roughly handled by the historians. Since that time the pendulum has swung the other way with a vengeance, and now he even has an Association to honour his memory.

'Mr. Lely,' said Cromwell when he sat for his portrait, 'I desire you would use all your skill to paint my picture truly like me, and not flatter me at all; but remark all these roughnesses, pimples, warts, and everything, otherwise I will never pay a farthing for it.' I have worked in the belief that he would have said much the same thing to his biographer.

ACKNOWLEDGMENT

Figures 5, 6, are reproduced by gracious permission of Her Majesty The Queen
The Author and Publishers also wish to thank the following for permission to reproduce the illustrations appearing in this book:
The Ashmolean Museum, for figs. 8, 11, 17, 26
The Lord Barnard, for fig. 14
The Trustees of the British Museum, for figs. 24, 27
The Duke of Buccleuch, for figs. 7, 25
The Trustees of the Chequers Trust and the Trustees of the Victoria and Albert Museum, for fig. 3
Mrs. J. H. Dent-Brocklehurst, for fig. 15
The Mansell Collection, for fig. 22
The National Portrait Gallery, for figs. 9, 12
Lieutenant-Colonel The Lord Saye and Sele, for fig. 10
The Master and Council of Sidney Sussex College, Cambridge, for fig. 1
The Publishers are unable to trace the owner of the portrait illustrated in fig. 13

CONTENTS

		Page
Preface		5
Acknowledgment		7
List of Illustrations		11
1	Early Days	13
2	Backbencher	22
3	Captain Cromwell and the Edgehill Campaign	32
4	Colonel Cromwell raises his Regiment	38
5	Gainsborough and Winceby	43
6	Ironsides: Lt.-General Cromwell and Marston Moor	49
7	Second Newbury and the Self-Denying Ordinance	57
8	The New Model	65
9	King, Parliament and Army	77
10	The Second Civil War and the Execution of King Charles	85

Page

11 Ireland, 1649–1650   93

12 Scotland, 1650   98

13 Worcester   106

14 The Last of the Rump   111

15 The Reluctant Dictator, 1653–1655   116

16 The Constable, 1655–1658   126

17 Cromwell as Soldier and Statesman   136

Select Bibliography   145

Index   147

LIST OF ILLUSTRATIONS

Figure

1 Cromwell
   From the portrait by Samuel Cooper   *Frontispiece*

2 Cromwell's signature as Protector, 1657   *Frontispiece*

                                                        facing page
3 'Oliver Cromwell aged two years'   14

4 Sidney Sussex College, Cambridge
   From the engraving in Cantabrigia Illustrata, *1688*   15

5 Elizabeth Steward: a miniature traditionally of
   Cromwell's mother
   From a contemporary miniature   28

6 Cromwell's favourite daughter:
   Mrs. Elizabeth Claypole
   From a contemporary miniature   28

7 Cromwell's wife: Elizabeth Bourchier
   From a miniature by Samuel Cooper   28

8 John Lilburne
   From a print dated 1641   29

9 John Pym
   From a woodcut by E. Bower, 1642   29

10 Colonel Nathaniel Fiennes
   From the portrait by Mirevelt   44

11 General John Lambert
   From a contemporary engraving   45

Figure   *facing page*

12   Richard Cromwell
       Detail from a contemporary portrait   45

13   Mrs. Ireton: Cromwell's eldest daughter,
       Bridget
       From the portrait by Sir Peter Lely   76

14   Sir Henry Vane the Younger
       From the portrait by Sir Peter Lely   77

15   General Henry Ireton, 1650
       From the portrait by Robert Walker   77

16   Cromwell's House: Clerkenwell Close   *page*   85

17   The Execution of Charles I
       From a contemporary print   92

18   The Battle of Dunbar, 1650
       Detail from a contemporary engraving by Payne Fisher   93

19   Cromwell's House in Whitehall   *page*   97

20   Medal to commemorate the Victory at Dunbar   *page* 105

21   Medal commemorating Blake's Victories   *page* 126

22   Cromwell expelling Parliament, 1653
       From a contemporary Dutch print   132

23   'The Lord Protector Lying in State . . .'
       From a contemporary print   132

24   The Great Seal of the Commonwealth, 1651
       Designed by Thomas Simon   133

25   Cromwell
       Detail from the unfinished miniature by Samuel Cooper   140

26   Cromwellian Gold 'Broad'   141

27   Second Great Seal of the Protector, 1655
       Designed by Thomas Simon   141

1 EARLY DAYS

I live . . . in Mesheck, which they say signifies *Prolonging*; in Kedar, which signifieth *Blackness*; . . .

'I WAS by birth a gentleman, living neither in any considerable height nor yet in obscurity. I have been called to several employments in the nation, and—not to be over-tedious—I did endeavour to discharge the duty of an honest man in those services to God and His people's interest, and to Commonwealth.' Thus the Protector in one of his later speeches spoke of his origin and the aims that he had set himself in his career.

That he was a gentleman is certain; as to his endeavours we must judge hereafter, for his character is a matter for controversy, and he remains to this day something of an enigma. For that reason it is as well to begin by establishing those facts about his background, education, tastes, and appearance which are not really in dispute.

The fortunes of the Cromwell family were built on the spoils of the monasteries, and Oliver's great-grandfather, Richard Williams, had taken the surname of his patron, Thomas Cromwell, Earl of Essex (1485?–1540). The Williams family originally came from Glamorgan. Oliver's father, Robert, had a small estate at Huntingdon worth about £300 a year—certainly not less than £3,000 per annum today[1]. He was M.P. for Huntingdon (1593) and a Justice of the Peace, a man of no particular distinction but a typical representative of the county families of his day. One of his sisters was the mother of John Hampden (1594–1643), and another of Major-General Edward Whalley, the regicide. Cromwell's mother, Elizabeth, was a Steward, tracing her ancestry to an old Norfolk family

---
[1] 1961.

of the unromantic name of Styward. The fortunes of the Stewards had also been founded on the ruins of the Roman Catholic Church, but by Oliver's time neither Stewards nor Cromwells were particularly prosperous for they had been prolific—Oliver Cromwell himself had seven sisters—and their inheritance had become dispersed.

Oliver's education, which was not otherwise remarkable, was thoroughly Puritan. The master at the Free School of Huntingdon when he was there was the Reverend Thomas Beard (d.1632), author of *The Theatre of God's Judgments*, who believed that the Pope was Antichrist, and that crime never goes unpunished in this world or the next. When in 1616 Cromwell went up to Cambridge it was to Sidney Sussex, a college which William Laud, the future Archbishop, was to describe as 'a hotbed of Puritanism'. The chapel of Sidney Sussex had neither stained glass windows nor images and its services followed the Prayer Book only sufficiently to keep within the law. Its Master, the Calvinist Samuel Ward, was one of the translators of King James's Bible, the book to which Cromwell was to turn so often for ideas, ammunition and arguments to fortify his opinions; and to which the eloquence and forcefulness of his language owed so much.

Oliver did not distinguish himself either at school or university, but later he appreciated the value of education. In 1650 he advised his idle son Richard to study cosmography, mathematics, in which he himself is said to have excelled, and a little history. 'These fit for public services for which a man is born'. Like Montrose, Cromwell greatly valued Sir Walter Raleigh's *History of the World*: ''Tis a body of History, and will add much more to your understanding than fragments of story.' He had sufficient Latin to be able to converse with the Dutch Ambassador in that language when he was Protector. In his youth he delighted in 'horse and field exercise, football, cudgels and other manly sports'.

Maidstone, the steward of the Protector's household, tells us that he was about 5 feet 10 inches in height, and that he was

> well compact and strong, his head so shaped as you might see it a store-house and shop both of a vast treasury of natural parts. His temper was exceeding fiery, . . . but the flame of it, kept down for the most part, was soon allayed with those moral endowments he had. He was

Oliver Cromwell
aged 2 years

3 'OLIVER CROMWELL AGED TWO YEARS'
This contemporary portrait, it has been suggested, may be of the Protector's son

4 SIDNEY SUSSEX COLLEGE, CAMBRIDGE. CROMWELL'S ROOMS WERE IN HALL COURT, ON THE LEFT
From the engraving in David Loggan, 'Cantabrigia Illustrata', 1688

naturally compassionate towards objects in distress, even to an effemi-
nate measure. . . . A larger soul, I think, hath seldom dwelt in a
house of clay . . .

His eyes were blue or grey and his rugged countenance was
adorned by a nose of considerable proportions. 'If you prove false,
I will never trust a fellow with a big nose again', Sir Arthur Hesilrige once told him. He had in fact the robust physique of the gentleman farmer that he was, though in later life he suffered a good deal
from fevers, apparently of a malarial sort, which he may originally
have contracted in his native fenlands.

Despite his Puritanism Oliver 'loved an innocent jest', and though
his sense of humour was not very subtle, it was of a kind to appeal
to his soldiers. Baxter goes so far as to say: 'He was naturally of such
a vivacity, hilarity and alacrity, as another man is when he hath
drunken a cup of wine too much.' But Cromwell's temperament
was not as simple as that. Sir Theodore Mayerne, the famous London doctor, whom he consulted in 1628, described him in his case-
book as 'valde melancholicus', while Dr. Simcott, his physician at
Huntingdon, told Sir Philip Warwick 'that for many years his patient
was a most splenetic man, and had fancies about the cross in that
town; and that he had been called up to him at midnight and such
unseasonable hours very many times, upon a strong fancy, which
made him believe he was then dying'. It seems that, at least in his
early manhood, he was subject to fits of depression. Perhaps these
fancies fled away with the religious conversion which came to him
apparently in the 1630s.

Sometimes as Protector, as Bulstrode Whitelocke tells us, he 'by
way of diversion would make verses with us, and everyone must try
his fancy. He commonly called for tobacco, pipes, and a candle,
and would now and then take tobacco himself; . . . ' In his later
days he drank a small ale called 'Morning Dew', and sometimes a
light wine for his health. His diet was plain.

His dress too was usually plain. Warwick who saw him in Parliament in November 1640 describes him:

> The first time, that ever I took notice of him, was in the very beginning
> of the Parliament held in November 1640, when I vainly thought my-
> self a courtly young gentlemen: . . . I came one morning into the House

well clad, and perceived a gentleman speaking . . . very ordinarily ap-
parelled; for it was a plain cloth suit, which seemed to have been made
by an ill country tailor; his linen was plain, and not very clean; and I
remember a speck or two of blood upon his little band which was not
much larger than his collar; his hat was without a hatband: his stature
was of a good size, his sword stuck close to his side, his countenance
swollen and reddish, his voice sharp and untunable and his eloquence
full of fervour . . .

a legacy perhaps from his Welsh ancestors. When he dismissed the
Long Parliament he was wearing plain black clothes with grey worsted stockings, and in December 1653 we find him dressed in a plain
black suit and cloak. Warwick tells us that, when he was Protector,
Cromwell got a better tailor, and speaks of his 'great and majestic
deportment and comely presence'. Entertained by the Lord Mayor
in 1654 he appeared in a musk-coloured suit, and a coat richly em-
broidered with gold. He was no longer the uncouth country gentleman of 1640.

His favourite sports were hunting and hawking, and as late as 1654
he 'coursed and killed a fat buck' in Hampton Court Park. It was
noted that his guest, the Swedish Ambassador, 'would not adventure
to leap ditches after the Protector, but was more wary'. Oliver was
also fond of singing and instrumental music.

Despite the Puritan influences to which he was early exposed, his
intense piety was a slow growth. Baxter describes him as 'a prodigal
in his youth', while Warwick alleges that: 'The first years of his manhood were spent in a dissolute course of life in good fellowship and
gaming, which afterwards he seemed very sensible of and sorrowful
for'. By 1638 he himself could write: 'You know what my manner
of life hath been. Oh, I lived in darkness and hated light. I was a chief
—the chief of sinners. This is true; I hated Godliness, yet God had
mercy on me.'

The Puritans fall into two main groups, Independents and
Presbyterians, and Cromwell belonged to the former. The
Presbyterians modelled their church government on the Genevan
pattern which had been introduced into Scotland by John
Knox. The Independents were less rigid and were organized in
autonomous congregations. Both Puritan parties were united,
however, in regarding the Bishops of the Established Church as
'dregs of popery'.

So much for Oliver's background, education, physique, temperament, health, appearance and tastes as testified by friend and foe. Yet knowing so much we still know little. We must examine his achievements as soldier and statesman, endeavouring to estimate his character: cruel or compassionate; sanctimonious or sincere; devious or downright—or each in turn. In February 1629 he was elected to represent Huntingdon in the third Parliament of King Charles I. The Cromwells had been losing ground in the county. In 1627 Sir Oliver, to pay his debts, had sold Hinchinbrooke House to Sir Sidney Montague, whose family thereafter took the lead in the affairs of Huntingdonshire. Cromwell's election, therefore, probably owed as much to his own character and reputation as to family influence.

In this assembly, in which one of the lords estimated the Commons could buy the upper house thrice over, Cromwell was a very inconsiderable person and played a very inconspicuous part. He was no doubt in his place to hear Sir John Eliot urge the importance of what was at stake: 'Upon this dispute not only our goods and lands are engaged, but all that we call ours. Those rights, those privileges that made our fathers freemen are in question.' The Petition of Right declared that arbitrary imprisonment and taxation without the consent of Parliament were illegal.

It is significant that Oliver's only reported speech in this Parliament was on a religious topic. He spoke on behalf of the free preaching of Puritan doctrine, and against the silence which the King sought to impose on religious controversy. This, probably his maiden speech, was made when the House was discussing charges against Dr. Richard Neile, the Bishop of Winchester. Neile had reprimanded Oliver's old master, Beard, for a sermon against Dr. William Alabaster who, according to Cromwell, had 'preached flat Popery' at Paul's Cross.

This was Cromwell's contribution to the Puritan assault of Pym and Eliot on the religious policy of the King. Before the attack could be driven home Charles, who, like his father before him, believed in the maxim, 'No bishop, no King', dissolved Parliament, contrasting the 'dutiful demeanours' of the Lords with 'the undutiful and seditious carriage in the lower house'.

For the next eleven years the King was to rule without a Parliament. During the years of prerogative government Cromwell played no great part in public life. There is some evidence that during this period he twice sided with the poorer members of the community. The first was when in 1630 the borough of Huntingdon obtained a new charter. Although Cromwell as a Justice of the Peace had consented to it, he later objected on the grounds that it enabled the aldermen to deal with the common property as they pleased to the detriment of the poorer townsmen. The Mayor complained of the strong language Cromwell had used and the latter was summoned to appear before the council. The dispute being referred to the Earl of Manchester, Cromwell owned that he had spoken in 'heat and passion' and apologized. Nevertheless the Earl upheld his objections and ordered that the charter should be altered to meet them.

Sir Philip Warwick alleges that Cromwell successfully opposed the King over the draining of the fens, and he may well have taken part in this dispute of 1636. Charles was in fact defending the rights of the Commoners against the Undertakers. Historians have supposed that this episode won Cromwell his nickname of 'Lord of the Fens', though this is first found in the Royalist newspaper, *Mercurius Aulicus*, in November 1643. The whole business is too obscure to prove very much, but a lingering impression remains that in some way Cromwell merited a certain popularity for standing up for the rights of the Commoners. It is reasonable to suppose that this stood him in good stead when he came to recruit a regiment some years later.

In 1631 he moved to St. Ives, where he lived for five years taking his part in local administration, but occupied for the most part with farming. There is a tradition that he usually frequented divine service, but if he still kept within the law in so far as the established Church was concerned, his Puritanism had now reached its full maturity. The astute Bishop of Lincoln already regarded him as a spokesman of sectaries, and a letter of 11 January 1636 survives in which Oliver urges a London friend to continue to provide for a nonconformist lecturer: 'I beseech you therefore in the bowels of Christ Jesus . . . let the good man have his pay.' Needless to say the suppression of lecturers of this sort was part of Archbishop Laud's ecclesiastical policy.

Heath, though usually unreliable, has a story of this period which appears to be founded on fact.

He was grown (that is he pretended to be) so just, and of so scrupulous a conscience, that having some years before won thirty pounds of one Mr. *Calton* at play, meeting him accidentally, he desired him to come home with him and to receive his money, telling him that he had got it by indirect and unlawful means, and that it would be a sin in him to detain it any longer; . . .

In 1636 Sir Thomas Steward, Cromwell's uncle, died leaving him the bulk of his estate. Cromwell moved to Ely, where he lived at the glebe house which was to be his home until he moved to London in 1647. Oliver succeeded his uncle as farmer of the Cathedral tithes. Although his house at Ely was plain and unassuming he was now a man of property. Marvell thought of his quiet life at this time when he wrote:

> *From his private gardens, where*
> *He lived reservèd and austere,*
> *As if his highest plot*
> *To plant the bergamot.*

But if England was at peace, in Germany Catholic and Protestant had long been engaged in a devastating and brutal war. Firth has made the point that 'to the Puritan farmer, prescient of a future struggle, the war was not merely a spectacle but a military education'. It is indeed likely that he devoured *The Swedish Intelligencer* if it came his way.

And quiet though Ely may have been, stirring events were doing nearer home than Lützen and Breitenfeld. In June 1637, Prynne, Burton and Bastwick were tried by the court of Star Chamber for circulating libels upon the bishops. They were condemned to be pilloried, to lose their ears and to suffer solitary confinement for life. The courage of the victims stirred the pity and indignation of a great crowd whose angry roars could easily be heard as far away as Whitehall—heard by a King who had no soldiers to disperse the mob his policy had brought together.

It was now too that 'Freeborn John' Lilburne began his long career of defiance to arbitrary government. Brought before Star Chamber he refused to take the oath to answer all questions put to him by the court. For this, though a gentleman by birth, he was whipped at the cart's tail from the Fleet Prison to Palace Yard, pilloried and gagged, and later wellnigh starved in prison. The echoes of such cases travelled far beyond Ely.

The next great case in this crucial year touched Cromwell more nearly for his cousin, John Hampden, was the defendant and Oliver St. John, a relative by marriage, was Hampden's counsel.

Ship Money was the most fruitful of the various expedients by which the King endeavoured to finance his government during the years of personal rule. In so far as the coast towns were concerned there was precedent for it. But in 1635 and 1636 all were called upon to contribute; it was being transformed into a permanent source of revenue. When signs of resistance became visible the King asked the judges whether he had the right to command his subjects to furnish ships for the defence of the Kingdom in times of danger. They replied in the affirmative, but John Hampden—a very wealthy man— refused to pay. The case was tried before twelve judges and despite St. John's eloquence, the Crown won by seven voices to five. But the judges did more harm than good to their master's cause. There was no limit to the power of the Crown over the person and the purses of freeborn Englishmen, if absolute monarchy had a legal basis. We cannot doubt that Cromwell studied the case with more than ordinary interest, but there is no evidence that he, too, refused to pay.

While the legal-minded English were digesting Ship Money and swallowing as best they could Archbishop Laud's attempts by his visitations to bring 'the beauty of holiness' into church services, their northern neighbours had worked themselves into a frenzy over Charles's insistence that Scotland should accept the book of Common Prayer. Charles refused all conciliation. The Scots appointed commissioners, who became in effect their rulers, and in March 1638 with great unanimity subscribed to the Solemn League and Covenant for the defence of their religion. Charles's attempt to reduce them by force of arms—the First Bishops' War (1639)—foundered for three main reasons. There was neither the money to finance a war, nor the army to wage it, nor yet the will to win it.

In all this Cromwell played no active part. But if he was still chiefly preoccupied with the state of his own soul, he seems to have sensed that the time was not far off when he would be called upon to serve and to suffer for the honour of God. Writing on 13 October 1638 to a beloved cousin, Mrs. St. John, he expresses his inmost thoughts:

Truly, then, this I find; That He giveth springs in a dry and barren wilderness where no water is. I live . . . in Mesheck, which signifies *Prolonging*; in Kedar, which signifieth *Blackness*: yet the Lord forsaketh me not. Though He do prolong, yet He will (I trust) bring me to His tabernacle, to His resting-place. My soul is with the congregation of the first-born, my body rests in hope, and if here I may honour my God either by doing or by suffering, I shall be most glad.

Truly no poor creature hath more cause to put forth himself in the cause of his God than I. I have had plentiful wages beforehand, and I am sure I shall never earn the least mite. . . . He it is that enlighteneth our blackness, our darkness. . . . One beam in a dark place hath exceeding much refreshment in it. Blessed be His name for shining upon so dark a heart as mine! You know what my manner of life hath been. Oh, I lived in and loved darkness, and hated the light. I was a chief, the chief of sinners. . . .

Cromwell lived to be 59. Now with only twenty years still to run, he stood at the threshold of his own middle-age and of his country's revolution. With relatively little experience of the great world or of affairs; with a comfortable fortune—but certainly no more, for he had a wife and eight children to provide for; with an ordinary education; and some useful family connections; he was about to start upon his astonishing career as soldier and statesman.

One great asset he had. The follies of youth were behind him. Gambling he had certainly rejected, though depression could not be cast out so easily. It may not be too far-fetched to suppose that in speaking of 'Kedar, which signifieth *Blackness*' he was thinking of the melancholy, which Mayerne had once diagnosed. But his soul was now easier. He had had a glimpse of the light, more than he felt he merited. With all his responsibilities in this world, he sought refreshment only in the next. He was in a mood to welcome whatever duty or sacrifice might come his way. He was not to live in Mesheck much longer.

2 BACKBENCHER

That slovenly fellow . . . who hath no ornament in his speech; . . .

THE Short Parliament (5 April–5 May 1640), in which Cromwell sat as one of the members for Cambridge, was summoned by the King in order to finance the Second Bishops' War.

When Parliament opened, Pym, now the acknowledged leader of the opponents of the court, catalogued the grievances of the last fifteen years, asserting that 'the parliament is that to the commonwealth which the soul is to the body'. His speech was received with cries of 'A good oration!' and the Commons now took the attitude that 'till the liberties of the house and the Kingdom were cleared they knew not whether they had anything to give or no!' Even an offer to abandon the collection of Ship Money failed to induce them to vote funds. Expecting a petition against the Scots war, and convinced that money would not be forthcoming, Charles dissolved Parliament on 5 May. While this dismayed all moderate men it left the opposition leaders unmoved. St. John said that all was well: 'things must be worse before they could be better, and this Parliament would never have done what was necessary to be done'.

The Scots now crossed the Tyne and occupied Durham and Northumberland. There was nothing but their own good sense to prevent them advancing on London. 'The Short Parliament had been called to pay for the conquest of the Scots but its more famous successor was called to buy them out of England' (Trevelyan).

Cromwell was a person of some importance in the new Parliament which met on 3 November 1640. Only about a quarter of the members had sat in the Parliament of 1628, and he was one of them. His eleven close relations in the House included John Hampden and Oliver St. John, and he probably made one of the little group who kept a common table at Pym's lodging, Sir Richard Manley's house in a little court behind Westminster Hall. Though his activity was mostly displayed in committee he made a speech within a week of the assembly of Parliament—ironically enough on behalf of John Lilburne, who was to be such a thorn in his flesh in later life.

Lilburne sought redress for his sufferings since his arrest in 1637. Warwick's description of Cromwell's appearance on this occasion has already been quoted. It seems he was no great speaker as yet

> —his voice sharp and untunable, and his eloquence full of fervour; for the subject matter could not bear much of reason; it being in behalf of a servant of Mr. Prynn's who had dispersed libels against the Queen for her dancing and suchlike innocent and courtly sports; and he aggravated the imprisonment of this man by the Council Table unto the height, that one would have believed the very Government itself had been in great danger by it. I sincerely profess it lessened much my reverence unto that great council for he was very much hearkened unto.

It may have been on this occasion that Lord Digby, then one of the 'opposition', asked Hampden who Cromwell was, 'For I see he is of our side, by his speaking so warmly this day'. Hampden replied: 'That slovenly fellow which you see before us, who hath no ornament in his speech; I say that sloven, if we should ever come to have a breach with the King (which God forbid) in such case will be one of the greatest men of England.'

Hampden, it would seem, was no more impressed by Cromwell's oratory, or his tailor, than was Warwick, the Cavalier. Yet he, whom Clarendon thought of greater cunning and address than Pym himself, had already discerned hidden depths of character and talent in Oliver. One great asset Cromwell had. From the outset nobody had the least illusion as to which side he was on. His uncouth strength, his rude eloquence, were wholly at Pym's command.

The Courts of Star Chamber and High Commission, the Council of the North and the Council of Wales and the Marches were now swept away. By the Tonnage and Poundage Act it became illegal to levy customs duties without a Parliamentary grant. Ship Money was declared unlawful.

Still more important than these reforms was the passing of the Triennial Act which bound the King to call a Parliament every third year, and provided machinery in case he should omit to do so. Cromwell had a hand in this. It originated in a bill introduced by William Strode, to revive an old law of King Edward III's time by which a Parliament had to be summoned each year. Cromwell not only moved the second reading of this bill (30 December 1640), but he was one of the committee which framed the Act. Charles gave his assent on 15 February 1641, the same day that he agreed to the bill of attainder against Strafford. Had he not been distracted by the plight of his minister it is inconceivable that he would have passed this 'Act for the perpetual parliament', without protest.

So far the House had shown itself practically unanimous on constitutional matters. The same spirit did not prevail where religious questions were concerned. There were those like Nathaniel Fiennes and Sir Henry Vane who were for the abolition of Episcopacy, 'root and branch'. Beyond question Cromwell was with them from the first. His next recorded speech was on 9 February 1641. A Royalist member, Sir John Strangways, had defended the bishops on the grounds that they were 'one of the three estates of the kingdom and have a voice in Parliament'. This drew a violent outburst from Oliver. His opponents complained of his unparliamentary language, and moved that he should be called to the Bar of the House to apologize. But Pym and Denzil Holles came to his rescue. When Cromwell rose again, it was merely to pour fuel on the flames.

> He did not understand why the gentleman that last spoke (Strangways) should make an inference of parity from the Church to the Commonwealth; not that there was any necessity of the great revenues of Bishops. He was more convinced touching the irregularity of Bishops than ever before, because, like the Roman Hierarchy, they would not endure to have their condition come to a trial.

The matter was now allowed to drop, perhaps, as Abbott suggests, because his opponents did not wish 'to risk another outburst from this firebrand'.

In May the old dispute over the fen drainage raised its head again, and this time Cromwell certainly took the part of the 'poor commoners'. Hyde, writing some years later, describes the scene towards the end of June, when a committee, of which he was chairman, considered the petition of the inhabitants of Somersham, Huntingdonshire.

Lands had been enclosed and sold to the Earl of Manchester and his son, Lord Mandeville. Of this the inhabitants 'made loud complaints, as a great oppression'. Oliver Cromwell, one of the committee, 'ordered the witnesses and petitioners in the method of the proceeding; and seconded, and enlarged upon what they said, with great passion'. They

> who were a very rude kind of people, interrupted the counsel and witnesses on the other side, with great clamour, when they said anything that did not please them; so that Mr. Hyde . . . was compelled to use some sharp reproofs, and some threats, to reduce them to such a temper that the business might be quietly heard. Cromwell, in great fury, reproached the Chairman for being partial and [said] that he discountenanced the witnesses by threatening them.

When the committee supported Hyde, Cromwell, 'who was already too much angry', became more inflamed. He answered Lord Mandeville with 'so much indecency and rudeness', that nobody would ever have thought that one day they would fight on the same side.

In the end Hyde warned Cromwell that if he went on in the same way he would adjourn the committee and complain of him to the House. It is evident that Cromwell was as yet far from having that control of his temper which Maidstone credits him with as Protector. Like Sir Anthony Absolute, he was the most reasonable of men when he was not crossed.

In August the King set out for Scotland, a journey to which Pym and his party were strongly opposed, Cromwell being among those who voiced a protest. But Charles was playing into the hands of his enemies. In his absence a Committee of Defence, with Pym at its head, virtually governed the country. Parliament assumed the unprecedented powers of governing by ordinance without the concurrence of the King, and of levying money.

Cromwell's activities later in the month included delivering to the House (28 August) petitions from prisoners in the Fleet and the King's Bench asking that, as formerly in times of pestilence, they might be allowed to go into the country on good bail. In September he spoke against the Common Prayer Book during the debate on the 'ordinance against Innovations in the Worship of God', a debate of great importance, for thenceforth Anglican and Nonconformist were clearly in opposite camps, however much they might agree on constitutional questions. Although the Root and Branch Bill to abolish Episcopacy had not been passed, the House agreed (8 September) to move communion tables from the east end of the churches, to take down the rails, and to remove all crucifixes and 'scandalous pictures' of the Trinity and the Virgin. Dancing and sports on the Sabbath were forbidden. Much as Oliver approved all this, his views on Church government were vague. Warwick tells us how two Episcopalian members asked him what system he wished to substitute for theirs. 'I can tell you, sirs, what I would not have; though I cannot, what I would.'

When the House reassembled for the autumn session England was experiencing something of a conservative reaction. As early as September the Venetian Ambassador had noted that Parliament was losing its great credit, since 'instead of relief it has brought expense and discomfort to the people'. The withdrawal of the Scottish army had, of course, greatly weakened Pym's position.

The Episcopalians, numerous if somewhat inarticulate, were alarmed by the rancour of the religious extremists, among whom Oliver must certainly be numbered. Many who could regard the Puritan onslaught against Laud's bishops with equanimity, were offended by the attack on their ritual. Sir Edward Nicholas, now a Secretary of State, could write that only the fear of popery now came between the King and his people.

Unhappily for Charles, any hope of a Royalist revival was now shattered by the dreadful news of the rebellion in Ireland. With Strafford's iron hand removed, the Irish decided that they were a free people, rose with a very fair degree of unanimity, and slaughtered several thousands of English Protestants. The pamphleteers recorded and invented the usual atrocities—ravished women, toasted children and mutilated men. It was all too commonly believed that the rebels were acting in the King's name. One of the Irish leaders exhibited a commission, 'under the broad seal of England', authorizing the restoration of the Roman Catholic religion. When the news came both parties at once agreed to reconquer Ireland, paying for the task by confiscating Irish land. Popery was to be tolerated nowhere in His Majesty's dominions. When Members and London merchants subscribed funds for the campaign Cromwell gave £500, probably about a year's income. It was a big sum to spend on a country of which he knew next to nothing.

With an army raising for Ireland the question of control was bound to arise. If it was left in the King's hands, none could say where it would be employed. This Cromwell saw as clearly as any, and it was he that proposed on 6 November that the Earl of Essex should command all the trained bands south of Trent until further order. Pym, meanwhile, feeling that he was losing ground, had been preparing an appeal to the people, the Grand Remonstrance. This bill was a long catalogue of the wrongs suffered by the nation during King Charles's reign—not forgetting the old fen dispute which Cromwell was to explain—and suggestions for reform. To the Royalists the Remonstrance was sedition. To Pym and his followers, despite the fact that they had already secured so many of the reforms they sought, it was of vital importance. Cromwell told Lord Falkland afterwards 'that if the Remonstrance had been rejected he would have sold all he had the next morning, and never have seen England more; and he knew there were many other honest men of the same resolution'.

Nevertheless he was confident of the outcome; indeed he quite underestimated the strength of the opposition to this indictment. When its opponents asked for time to consider the charges, Clarendon tells us that Cromwell, 'who at that time was little taken notice of', told Falkland that the debate would be 'A very sorry one', supposing few would oppose it. But in fact it lasted for about fifteen hours (22 November), and was so bitterly contested that Sir Philip Warwick half expected bloodshed in the House:

> . . . at three of the clock in the morning, when they voted it, I thought, we had all sat in the valley of the shadow of death; for we, like Joab's and Abner's young men, had catcht at each other's locks, and sheathed our swords in each other's bowels, had not the sagacity and great calmness of Mr. Hampden by a short speech prevented it, and led us to defer our angry debate, until the next morning.

Eventually, with half the members absent, the Remonstrance was carried by eleven votes (159–148). Pym and his friends had 'provided that not a man of their party was absent, . . .' (Clarendon).

If the Grand Remonstrance was passed without bloodshed, it certainly brought war a step nearer, for the Royalists would not quietly accept the ecclesiastical policy set forth in its clauses.

The King returned from Scotland on 25 November more popular than when he went away. He was determined to make no further concessions, yet, had he been capable of watching and waiting for a space, Lords and Commons might well have done his work for him by falling out among themselves. Events, such as the printing of the Remonstrance—contrary to all previous practice—and the bill to nominate a lord general with powers to raise men and money and execute martial law, all conspired to exhaust his patience.

Charles was determined to rid himself of the Parliamentary leaders. He first removed the guards round the House and attempted to secure the Tower by making a trusted officer its lieutenant. All this was nothing to what followed. Pym had let it leak out that the Commons intended to impeach the Queen. Charles, enraged by this threat, as doubtless he was intended to be, decided to impeach five members, Pym, Hampden, Strode, Hesilrige and Holles, together with Lord Mandeville. On the afternoon of 4 January, since the Commons refused to give up the members, the King came to Westminster with 400 Cavaliers at his heels, to arrest them in person. This action had not the merit of being either constitutional, or wise, or successful. Pym knew well enough what was afoot, and long before the King's slow-moving procession could arrive, the five were on their way to the City.

Cromwell no doubt was in his place to hear the King's armed followers march through Westminster Hall, and upstairs into the lobby; to see the door flung open and the King, bidding his followers remain outside on pain of death, enter the chamber. As Charles walked to the Speaker's chair the members stood silent. Never before in its long history had the King entered the House.

'Mr. Speaker', said the King, 'I must for a time make bold with your chair.' Then, after explaining briefly why he was come: 'Is Mr. Pym here?' Turning to Lenthall he demanded if the five members were present. The Speaker, falling on his knees, uttered a reply which has deservedly become immortal:

'I have neither eyes to see nor tongue to speak in this place, but as this House is pleased to direct me.'

'Tis no matter', the King retorted, ' I think my eyes are as good as another's.' They swept the benches for a time, the members standing in deadly silence. 'All my birds have flown', he said at last, and departed whence he came 'in a more discontented and angry passion than he came in', followed by cries of 'Privilege! Privilege!' in

5 ELIZABETH STEWARD: A MINIATURE
TRADITIONALLY OF CROMWELL'S MOTHER
*Reproduced, by gracious permission of H. M.
The Queen, from a contemporary miniature*

6 CROMWELL'S FAVOURITE DAUGHTER:
MRS. ELIZABETH CLAYPOLE
*Reproduced, by gracious permission of H. M.
The Queen, from a contemporary miniature*

7 CROMWELL'S WIFE
ELIZABETH BOURCHIER
From a miniature by Samuel Cooper

8 JOHN LILBURNE
From a print dated 1641

9 JOHN PYM
From a woodcut by E. Bower, 1642

which, no doubt, the untunable voice of Cromwell joined as loud as the next man's.

When next day, still hoping to catch his birds, the King drove into the City, someone threw a paper into his coach with the heading 'To your tents, O Israel'. On 10 January Charles left Whitehall, and the next day the five members returned in triumph to Westminster. After the failure of the attempt to arrest them, civil war was perhaps inevitable. Yet the most sanguine Royalist can have seen but little hope that the King could raise an army. The parliamentary leaders, on the other hand, wasted no time in sending Sir John Hotham to seize Hull, with its great armouries. When Pym moved, on 14 January, that the House go into committee on the state of the kingdom, it was Cromwell that asked for a committee 'to consider of means to put the Kingdom in a posture of defence'. The 'breach with the King' of which Hampden and Digby had spoken, had now come, and Cromwell, however slow he may have been to make up his mind in later crises, was quite clear that this meant war. The same day the Houses issued a general order to the sheriffs to secure all stores of arms.

By declaring on the seventeenth that the attempt on the five members 'by soldiers, Papists and others' was 'a high breach of the privilege of Parliament, a great scandal to His Majesty and his government, a seditious act manifestly tending to the subversion of the Kingdom', the Commons virtually gave notice that they and not the King were the sovereign power.

The House now proceeded to exercise its newly assumed powers with all the zeal of the Star Chamber it had swept away. On 17 January Cromwell and his brother-in-law, Valentine Walton, 'informed the House of dangerous words spoken by a Huntingdonshire gentleman'. This was a Mr. Ravenscroft, a J.P. 'It had been witnessed against him under a minister's hand that he had said that if the King and Parliament should differ, the most of the gentry would be for the King, and that he had 1000 to assist him.'

Like all revolutionary bodies, Parliament was now excessively sensitive to criticism. Sir Edward Dering had published a pamphlet: 'A collection of Speeches . . . in the Matter of Religion'. He had voted against the Grand Remonstrance and had urged the retention of the bishops. On 2 February 1642 Cromwell moved that this book should be burnt by the sheriffs of London and Middlesex. Though his motion was carried, Oliver was not satisfied, because the book had come out some time before and obviously all the copies could not be called in. It was in this book that Dering noted that the Root and Branch Bill had been handed to him by 'S.A.H. and O.C.',[1] which may account for Oliver's eagerness to suppress it. Perhaps it is not unreasonable to suggest that private malice as well as the public good prompted him in this instance.

Cromwell had played a significant part during the pre-war period of the Long Parliament, but it must be assessed with caution. That he was whole-heartedly with Pym and Hampden is not in question. If he was not one of the five members, nor was St. John or Vane. He had been to the fore in the attack on the bishops, he had been one of the committee that drafted the Triennial Act, he had had some part in framing the Grand Remonstrance, and he had been instrumental in procuring the release of Prynne and others.

We do not know what Pym thought of him. If Hampden and Warwick were agreed as to his appearance, the former clearly thought more of his ability. Hyde seems to have been chiefly impressed by his passionate temper, while Digby too noted his 'warmth'. It is evident that he was more interested in the ecclesiastical than the constitutional questions which came before the House. By pressing the attack on the Episcopalians he played his part in driving the Anglicans into the ranks of the Cavaliers, and since without them the King could not have fought the civil war, Cromwell was in a sense one of those responsible for the strife that followed.

By early 1642 this hot-tempered, uncouth, energetic, forthright— even vindictive—middle-aged country gentleman had won himself a place in the second rank of the Parliamentarian leaders.

*   *   *

If Cromwell himself saw that war was inevitable and if, as Clarendon puts it, Pym and his friends 'fell to raising of monies under pretence of the relief of Ireland' while really preparing to fight the King, yet the majority of Englishmen were slow to realize what lay ahead. It was five generations since the roads and fields of England rang with 'stern alarums'. But gradually others were also coming

[1] Sir Arthur Hesilrige and Oliver Cromwell.

round to the view that war was unavoidable. On 5 March Cromwell reported to the House that a Colonel Francis Edmunds, an Irishman, had lately spoken 'dangerous words'. He had said that he wished that the King would 'raise his standard and maintain his prerogative by force of arms, and that if he knew where Pym, Hampden and Strode were, he would ease the King of further trouble from them'.

On 29 March Cromwell delivered a certificate from some Monmouthshire ministers showing that the strength of Papists was so great around Monmouth that they feared 'if some speedy course were not taken it would be in as great danger shortly as Ireland'. Pym had received a letter from the Mayor of Monmouth assuring him that the county magazine was safer there than at Newport, but this was not accepted and the unfortunate Mayor was commanded to appear before the House. Not a shot had been fired as yet, but now that King Pym ruled at Westminster, a man had but to be denounced to be ordered to undertake a journey of 130 miles and to appear before the House—with every prospect of finding himself lodged in the Fleet or some equally salubrious place as 'a malignant'. So much for the liberty of the subject.

On 27 May the King, now at York, issued a proclamation forbidding the trained bands or militia to muster without his consent. To this the 300 members of the Commons and the thirty Lords still at Westminster answered with their ultimatum, the Nineteen Propositions. They claimed control of the army and navy; of foreign and ecclesiastical policy; the appointment of ministers, councillors and judges, the right to punish or to pardon. Perhaps it was Pym's intention to make the quarrel irreconcilable by these demands, a sinister suggestion, but not altogether incredible, for he was sufficiently astute to see that open war might be the outcome. Ludlow, one of the most honest men on the Parliamentarian side, thought 'The question in dispute between us and the King's party was . . . whether the King should govern as a god by his will and the nation be governed by laws made by themselves, and live under a government from their own consent.' But absolutism had had its day when Strafford went to the Tower. It is hard to believe that after the first session of the Long Parliament Charles could ever have put the clock back to 1640, far less to 1629.

Be that as it may, the decisive factor now was to be the King's interpretation of the Nineteen Propositions, for on that depended the great question of peace or war.

> These being passed [came his stately response], we may be waited upon bareheaded, we may have our hand kissed, the style of majesty continued to us, and the King's authority declared by both Houses of Parliament may still be the style of your commands, . . . but as to true and real power we should remain but the outside, but the picture, but the sign of a King.

And so it came to pass that the Member for Cambridge left his seat at Westminster, took leave of his wife, seven of his eight children and his aged mother at Ely, and went to take part in the 'war without an enemy'. He had sixteen years to run and much of the next nine were to be spent in field and camp. At last he had the chance to honour his God by doing.

3 CAPTAIN CROMWELL AND THE EDGEHILL CAMPAIGN

. . . a plain russet-coated captain that knows what he fights for, and loves what he knows . . .

CAPTAIN OLIVER CROMWELL rode off to the wars to fight for one thing above all: Liberty of Conscience. With him, unlike many of the Parliamentarians, the curbing of the royal authority, albeit important, was a secondary consideration.

At the age of 43—a little on the old side for a troop commander— with no military experience either practical or theoretical, and, so far as we know, no veteran of the Dutch service to teach his troop 'the discipline of the wars', he was embarking on a new and exacting career. But he was a healthy man, fond of an outdoor life, sustained by his faith. He knew the sort of men he wanted in his troop—'the godly'—and he was a good judge of a horse. In an army of amateurs he had some assets, for 'in the country of the blind the one-eyed man is King'.

The Parliamentarians conducted the war through the agency of a Committee of Lords and Commons for the Safety of the Kingdom. This sat in London and governed the strategy of its various armies by remote control. They had a Commander-in-Chief, the Earl of Essex, who held the rank of Captain-General, though in practice he merely acted as the commander of their main field army. The Royalists governed their affairs through a Council of War with a predominantly military composition. Essex had previous military experience, as had Balfour and Skippon, but Bedford and Peterborough and many of the Parliamentarian regimental commanders had never heard a shot fired.

There was no standing army at this period, except in Ireland, but armies had been raised to fight the Scots in 1639 and 1640, and although there had been little action, those who had taken part must have learned something of drill, discipline and camp-life. On the Continent there were altogether eight English regiments of foot in the Dutch, French and Spanish services. Many officers had fought in the Thirty Years War, and numbers of these now came home. Still, the professional talent available, even on the Royalist side, was not nearly sufficient to go round. The campaign of 1642 was fought by armies of amateurs.

Cavalry was the most important arm at this period. The men were for the most part armed with a sword and a pair of pistols. Ordinarily their defensive armour consisted of back and breast plates, pot helmet and a buff coat. Cuirassiers, or 'Lobsters' in three-quarter armour were not unknown. Only in the Scots army were there lancers. Regiments usually consisted of six or more troops and numbered about 300 to 500 men. Pairs of troops often formed 'divisions' or squadrons. The men were generally drawn up for battle in three ranks, but one finds several instances of the Parliamentarians fighting six deep. In 1642 a troop consisted of a captain, a lieutenant, a cornet, a quartermaster, three corporals, two trumpeters, a sadler, a farrier, and sixty horse. The cornet carried the standard of the troop.

Cavalry is an arm designed for shock action. The great cavalry commanders of history have taught their men to charge home at the gallop, sword in hand, without using their firearms—at least until the enemy was broken. When the Civil Wars began, cavalry tactics varied according to the ideas of the commanders. Prince Rupert quickly taught his regiments the true method; others contented themselves with trotting about blazing away with their firearms, or, even worse, sat still and received their enemy with carbine and pistol, thus throwing away the advantage given by the impetus of their chargers. Basically the cavalry of the Civil Wars were equipped much like the cuirassiers of Napoleon's time or the Lifeguards of today.

One last point must be remembered about cavalry. It takes a long time to train them. Not every trooper who enlists is a born horseman, nor will he necessarily know how to care for his mount. It is not easy to teach the horses to stand straight in the ranks. An unruly horse may run away with his rider, however much that warrior may wish to rejoin his troop at the end of a *mêlée*. It takes time to teach men to ride in a troop, keeping their dressing by the cornet in the centre of the front rank, and keeping a horse's length between each rank. Outpost duty has to be learned, the men have to be taught to rally after a charge. Let us not be surprised if we discover strange things happening on the battlefields of the Civil War! Cromwell's own early service was all in the mounted arm.

Infantry regiments were in theory 1,200 strong, and had ten companies. One-third of the common soldiers were pikemen and the rest musketeers. The pikemen carried a pike 16 or 18 feet in length and a sword. They wore a helmet, breast and back plates and tassets to guard the thighs, and were, therefore, far from mobile. The musketeers were mostly armed with matchlocks, though a few already had early flintlocks. Their effective range was not more than 100 yards, and their rate of fire was very slow, perhaps no more than one round every three minutes.

The characteristics of such infantry compelled them to draw up in a deep formation, usually six or eight or even ten ranks deep, with the pikes in the centre. In this way the musketeers could keep up a rolling fire, and could take cover in the intervals of the pikemen if threatened by cavalry.

Artillery was invaluable for sieges, but seldom played a decisive part in the battles of the period. There were various reasons for this. One was the slow rate of fire of mid-seventeenth-century guns. Even if field guns could manage, say, one round in five minutes, it is obvious that one would need very many to do decisive damage. And numbers of guns were not available. The equipment was heavy, requiring many horses or oxen.

Range was no great problem since armies drew up near each other in those days. In practice even heavy guns would seldom fire at ranges over 1,000 yards. Mortars firing a primitive shell already existed and were very useful in a siege. The ordinary cannon fired caseshot or roundshot. At the beginning of the war, since the Parliament controlled the magazines of Hull and the Tower as well as most of the main ports, the Roundhead soldiers were much better armed than the Cavaliers, though not perhaps as well mounted.

★   ★   ★

On 15 August 1642 Sir Philip Stapleton reported to the House of Commons that Cromwell had seized the magazine in Cambridge Castle, and had prevented the University sending its plate to the King. With the aid of Valentine Walton he had effectually secured Cambridgeshire for the Parliament. This was Cromwell's first success in the Civil War—a war whose first shots had been fired in July at Hull, although the King was not to raise his Standard until 22 August.

It seems strange now that Cromwell should have gone through the 1642 campaign as a mere captain of horse. He was of a good enough age to be a colonel; he did not lack family influence among the leaders of the popular party; he had been active both in the House and in committee; he had spent his private fortune freely in the cause. Despite all this, it seems that he had as yet to make his mark with Pym, that he was looked on as a reliable and zealous supporter but not a born leader. The life he had led in peacetime had given insufficient scope to his talents. In August 1642 his powers of organization were still unappreciated by most of the leaders of his own side.

The officers of Cromwell's troop included Quartermaster John Desborough, his brother-in-law. Oddly enough, his eldest surviving son, Oliver, was not in his own troop, but was cornet to Lord St. John. Cromwell was voted £1,104 'mounting money' and proceeded to raise men and horses in Cambridgeshire and Huntingdon. By 29 August he could already muster sixty men, and on 8 September Quartermaster Desborough received a month's pay for the troop.

To this period probably belongs Warwick's story that he visited his old uncle and godfather, Sir Oliver Cromwell, at Ramsey 'with a good strong party of horse, and that he asked him his blessing, and that the few hours he was there, he would not keep on his hat in his presence; but at the same time he not only disarmed, but plundered him: for he took away all his plate'.

From the first, according to Richard Baxter,

> he had special care to get religious men into his troop. These men were of greater understanding than common soldiers and therefore more apprehensive of the importance and consequence of war and making not money but that which they took for the public felicity to be their end, they were the more engaged to be valiant. . . . These things it's probable Cromwell understood, . . . But yet I conjecture that . . . it was the very esteem and love of religious men that principally moved him; and the avoiding of those disorders, mutinies, plunderings and grievances of the country which deboist [debauched] men in armies are commonly guilty of. By this means he indeed sped better than he expected. Aires, Desborough, Berry, Evanson and the rest of that troop did prove so valiant that as far as I can learn they never once ran away before an enemy.

We cannot be certain when Cromwell reached the army. His troop was not one of those routed by Prince Rupert at Powick Bridge, near Worcester, on 23 September.

On 12 October the Royalist army, which had been concentrating at Shrewsbury, began its advance on London. Essex, who would have been wiser to post himself at Warwick, was at Worcester and so the King stole a march on him. The two armies, as yet inexpert, had little idea of each other's movements and when eventually their quartermasters clashed near Kineton the Royalists were nearer London than the Parliamentarians.

On 23 October a battle was fought at Edgehill. On the Royalist right Prince Rupert swept Ramsay's cavalry and a whole brigade of foot from the field, and most of his men, including his second line under Sir John Byron, galloped off in pursuit of the panic-stricken enemy. On their left Wilmot routed one Parliamentarian regiment, but missed two others, possibly because they were drawn up behind their infantry. The Royalist infantry advanced, but were counterattacked by Balfour. They were now hard put to it to re-form their line, but the King himself steadied them; their cannon belched caseshot into the advancing Roundheads, and such cavalry as Rupert had rallied sufficed to counter-balance Balfour's tired, but victorious troopers.

The upshot was that the Cavaliers took seven guns and some seventy colours. Essex fell back to Warwick—strange strategy for the man who should have been defending London—while King Charles was able to occupy Oxford, which was to be his headquarters for the rest of the war. Thus the King had rather the better of this first battle. But had Byron had the wit to fall on the flank of the rebel foot instead of dashing off in pursuit, the war might have fallen dead at a stroke.

Nobody knows what part Cromwell played in these stirring events. We are told that he was one of those who were 'of the right wing and never stirred from their troops, but . . . fought till the last minute'. Yet in a letter accompanying this same despatch we find him among the fugitives driven from the field. Denzil Holles later accused him of 'keeping out of the field', while the Royalist Dugdale has a story that he 'got up into a steeple . . . and there discerning by a perspective glass the two wings of horse to be utterly routed, made such haste to be gone, that . . . he swing'd down by a Bell-rope and ran away with his troop'.

For what it is worth, my reconstruction of all this is that Cromwell, through no fault of his own, took but a slight part in the battle, because his quarters were far from the main body of the army. Hearing the guns he reconnoitred from a church—very sensible—and, reading the battle as best he could, went where he could be most useful. Captain John Fiennes, who arrived at Kineton only in time to meet the fugitives, 'gathered a pretty body upon a hill together and with them (there being Captain Keightlye's and Captain Cromwell's troops at length come to them also) he marched towards the town' [Kineton]. This body attached itself to Hampden's brigade, which was marching up to join Essex.

One thing is certain: Cromwell saw enough of the rout to realize the shortcomings of Essex's army. In a speech of 1657 he said:

At my first going into this engagement, I saw our men were beaten at every hand . . . and I told him [John Hampden] I would be serviceable to him in bringing such men in as I thought had a spirit that would do something in the work. . . . 'Your troopers', said I, 'are most of them

old decayed servingmen and tapsters and such kind of fellows; and',
said I, 'their troopers are gentlemen's sons, younger sons and persons of
quality; do you think that the spirits of such base and mean fellows will
be ever able to encounter gentlemen that have honour and courage and
resolution in them? . . . You must get men . . . of a spirit that is likely to
go on as far as gentlemen will go, or else I am sure you will be beaten
still . . . He was a wise and worthy person, and he did think that I talked
a good notion but an impracticable one.

The King failed to exploit his victory at Edgehill by a rapid advance on London. When on 12 November his men stormed Brentford, Essex was already back in the capital. With his army swollen
by the London Trained Bands the Earl could muster such an array
that the battle of Turnham Green was never fought. Thus tamely
ended the campaign of Edgehill.

4   COLONEL CROMWELL
RAISES HIS REGIMENT

The Lord of the Fens

In December the armies went into winter quarters. The Edgehill
campaign had been indecisive: both sides began to prepare for a
long war, and to secure what territory they could. Men like Henry
Hastings and Richard Bagot left the King's 'Oxford' army to try to
hold down the Midlands; Cromwell and Ireton quitted Essex's
ranks to serve in the army of the newly formed Eastern Association.

Cromwell's main task was now to turn his troop into a regiment,
and by September 1643 he had managed to raise ten troops, besides
taking part in several operations. We already know something of
the kind of men he sought, from the famous conversation with
Hampden and from Baxter's comments. In the words of Bulstrode
Whitelocke they were 'most of them freeholders and freeholders'
sons, . . . who upon a matter of conscience engaged in this quarrel'.
But men of the traditional officer class did not come forward in

sufficient numbers to lead them, as we see from a letter of 29 August 1643 in which Cromwell, in forcible language, tells the Suffolk Commissioners his ideas on the subject of raising, training and controlling troops:

> I beseech you be careful what captains of horse you choose, what men be mounted; a few honest men are better than numbers. Some time they must have for exercise. If you choose godly honest men to be captains of horse, honest men will follow them, . . . I had rather have a plain russet-coated captain *that knows what he fights for, and loves what he knows*,[1] than that which you call a gentleman and is nothing else. I honour a gentleman that is so indeed.

In a postscript he adds: 'If you send such men as Essex hath sent, it will be to little purpose. Be pleased to take care that such may come along with them as will be able to bring them to the main body; and then I doubt not but we shall keep them, and make good use of them.' But if Cromwell was well content with his 'godly, precious men', there were many of his own party who looked askance at his methods of selection. A Presbyterian officer of dragoons in Manchester's army wrote:

> When any New Englishman or some new upstart Independent did appear there must be a way made for them by cashiering others, some honest commander or other, and those silly people put in their command. If you look upon his own regiment of horse see what a swarm there is of those that call themselves the godly; some of them profess they have seen visions and had revelations.

A letter of Cromwell's to the Suffolk committee (28 September 1643), written, of course, *before* his quarrel with Manchester, gives a partial answer to these charges:

> It had been well that men of honour and birth had entered into these employments, but why do they not appear? Who would have hindered them? But seeing it was necessary the work must go on, better plain men than none, but best to have men patient of wants, faithful and conscientious in the employment, and such, I hope, these will approve themselves to be. [In the same month he wrote of his regiment]: My troops increase, I have a lovely company; you would respect them, did you know them. They are no Anabaptists, but honest, sober Christians; they expect to be used as men.

[1] Author's italics.

It is important not to exaggerate this question of the social stand-ing of Cromwell's officers, for if James Berry, his Captain-Lieuten-ant, had been a clerk in a Shropshire ironworks, and if Robert Swallow and Ralph Margery were not gentlemen by birth, Major Whalley was his cousin, and Captain Valentine Walton his nephew. Henry Ireton came of an old Nottinghamshire family and had been educated at Trinity College, Oxford.

Marauding and pillage were abhorrent to Cromwell, and al-though he encouraged iconoclasm, in every other respect he main-tained strict, even severe, discipline from the first. To quote *Special Passages* (9–16 May): 'no man swears but he pays his twelve pence; if he be drunk he is set in the stocks, or worse, if one calls the other "Roundhead" he is cashiered; insomuch that the countries where they come leap for joy of them, and come in and join with them. How happy were it if all the forces were thus disciplined'. In April Cromwell had two deserters whipped in the market-place at Hunt-ingdon and 'turned off as renegadoes'.

Pay and good discipline go hand in hand. Without pay the most pious troops will pillage. Marauding is bound to sap the discipline of any army. Cromwell's difficulties were increased by the repeated failure of the local committees to provide money, for he was not wealthy enough to pay his men out of his own pocket, as a letter of 28 May to the Mayor of Colchester shows:

> I beseech you, hasten the supply to us; forget not money. I press not hard, though I do so need that, I assure you, the foot and dragooners are ready to mutiny. Lay not too much upon the back of a poor gentle-man, who desires, without much noise, to lay down his life, and bleed the last drop to serve the Cause and you. . . . I desire to deny myself; but others will not be satisfied.

These eloquent phrases brought little response, and Cromwell was compelled to pay the Essex men with £100 borrowed from the Mayor of Nottingham. His financial difficulties were only ended when he was appointed Governor of Ely (July 1643). Ireton, his deputy, levied great sums of money, 'pretending he would fortify the Isle', and the dragoon captain already quoted learned from the trea-surer that he collected £15,000 in the next eleven months. 'These monies were raised some by ordinance of Parliament, some other ways.' Not all this money was in fact spent on the fortifications;

Cromwell was concerned to make Ely as strong as possible, but no doubt part of the money collected went to pay his troops. The Presbyterian dragoon goes so far as to allege that he saw a letter from Oliver to the Committee at Ely: 'that they should pay to his wife £5 per week towards her extraordinaries, which hath been daily paid her a great while; I am sure there is no ordinance of Parliament for that.' This, however, was probably part of the pay due to Cromwell as Governor.

While his regiment was still raising Cromwell was active in other directions. He captured the Royalist mayor of Hertfordshire (January). He was active at Cambridge, not only in pressing on with the fortifications but in suppressing the Royalists. He 'caused the Heads of Houses to take down their organs and all the furniture of their chapels', and threatened to seize the rents of the Colleges.

On 14 March 1643 he suppressed a rising at Lowestoft; early in April he disarmed the Huntingdonshire Royalists. His next exploit was less creditable. He descended on Peterborough (22 April) where his men did considerable damage to the cathedral, burning books, and shattering the great west window. According to local tradition Oliver did not escape 'a finger of divine vengeance' on this occasion. Riding up some steps into the churchyard, his horse fell, and rising again suddenly, dashed his head against the lintels of the door, so that he 'fell to the ground as dead'. However this may be, he was well enough to be in action on 28 April, when he took part in the three-day siege of Crowland. The Royalist commander, Captain Cromwell, was one of at least six cousins who fought for the King. This seems to have been Oliver's first taste of active service since Edgehill, six months earlier, and his first experience of siege warfare.

The Cavaliers, part of the Marquis of Newcastle's Northern Army, had now concentrated at Newark and were threatening to invade the eastern counties. On 2 May the Commons ordered Cromwell and others to secure Lincolnshire. The next day we find him writing to the Committee of that county to explain why he had not yet done so, 'Though I know my heart is to assist you with all expedition'. Lord Grey, fearful of exposing Leicester to Henry Hastings, his active Royalist opponent, had failed to meet Cromwell at the appointed rendezvous, Stamford.

'Believe it', Cromwell writes, 'it were better, in my opinion,

Leicester were not than that there should not be an immediate taking of the field by your forces to accomplish the common end, wherein I shall deal as freely with him when I meet him as you can desire.' He had no exaggerated respect for the House of Peers.

After many delays and disappointments a Parliamentarian force under Lord Willoughby of Parham, Sir John Hotham and Cromwell concentrated at Sleaford on 9 May with the intention of attacking Newark, a fortress which was vital to the Royalists as a link between their Northern and Oxford armies. The Parliamentarians reached Grantham on 11 May and lingered about there for two days.

In the early hours of 13 May Lt.-General Charles Cavendish (1620–43) with some 1,200 men surprised three Roundhead troops in their quarters at Belton and practically destroyed them. He advanced again that evening and the two small armies faced each other within two miles of Grantham. Little is known of the action which followed: we owe such details as we possess to Cromwell himself. No report from Willoughby or Hotham, both of whom presumably outranked him, has survived.

> So soon as we had the alarm, we drew out our forces, consisting of about twelve troops, whereof some of them so poor and broken, that you shall seldom see worse. With this handful it pleased God to cast the scale. For after we had stood a little above musket-shot the one body from the other and the dragooners having fired on both sides for the space of half an hour or more, *they not advancing towards us, we agreed to charge them*,[1] and advancing the body after many shots on both sides, came on with our troops *a pretty round trot, they standing firm to receive us*;[1] and our men charging fiercely upon them, by God's providence they were immediately routed, and ran all away, and we had the execution of them two or three miles.

The Cavaliers lost 145 men while Cromwell estimates that the Parliamentarians 'lost but two men *at the most*'.[1] It is unlikely that the Roundheads were outnumbered on this occasion. *Special Passages*, a Roundhead newspaper, already credits Cromwell with 2,000 men, to these must be added Willoughby's men and also Hotham's.

The action is far from being a classic example of the handling of cavalry. Presumably the reason why the charge was not made at the gallop but at a fast trot, was that the men were firing as they went.

[1] Author's italics.

This hardly merits Oliver's description of 'charging fiercely', but one must remember that he was a comparatively inexperienced officer at this time: indeed this may actually have been his first charge. It may be noted in passing that so far from halting and re-forming after their success, the Roundheads pursued for two or three miles.

The fight contributed something to Oliver's military education no doubt, but the importance of this ill-conducted affair has been greatly exaggerated. But from one point of view, this success, won with so little loss, was of importance to Cromwell's new regiment. The men may have been under fire at Crowland, but for most of them it was their first mounted action. A regiment takes time to find itself, to shake down. A little bloodless victory the first time out is a great piece of luck for the commanding officer.

5 GAINSBOROUGH AND WINCEBY

. . . having good execution of them . . .

DURING the weeks that followed Grantham the Eastern Association achieved little or nothing, but in a letter of 13 June written to the Commissioners at Cambridge, Colonel Cromwell shows a common-sense grasp of their proper strategy. He wanted a regiment to be sent to the front and this is what he wrote:

> Let no words whatsoever lead your resolutions any other way, I maintain and affirm to you, as I would deal faithfully with you, and love the Association, two or three hundred men in those parts are enough. . . . If we be strong in the field, you are very well secured, and be assured if the enemy advance towards you we shall follow him in the heels . . . Let no words therefore from Sir John Palgrave prevail but command him to march up with all the volunteers . . . Service must be done. Command, you, and be obeyed! . . . We trust to endeavour our duties with these we have, but it will not be good to lose the use of any force God gives us, by negligence. The Lord give you, and us, zeal.

These home truths had their effect and Palgrave shortly took the field. But though his masters at Cambridge heeded Cromwell, Hotham had been carrying himself 'marvellous scornfully' towards him and Lord Grey of Groby. In a dispute over some oats he lost his head and turned guns on Cromwell. Essex ordered Hotham's arrest and Sir John Meldrum was sent to replace him. Escaping from Nottingham Castle, Hotham wrote to Speaker Lenthall that 'Colonel Cromwell had employed an anabaptist against him, and that one Captain White had been employed against him, who was lately but a yeoman. The valour of these men had only yet appeared in the defacing of churches'. Recaptured at Hull, which they had plotted to betray, Hotham, and his father, eventually paid for their treachery on the block.

These were dark days for the Parliament. On 18 June John Hampden was mortally wounded at Chalgrove Field, a heavy blow to the cause in general, and to Cromwell in particular.

On June 30 the Fairfaxes, lacking the help of their neighbours of the Eastern Association, were totally defeated by Newcastle at Adwalton Moor. In all Yorkshire only Hull held out. On 13 July the Queen's army, 4,500 strong, joined forces with the King, bringing a great train of arms and ammunition and enabling him to hold his own against Essex. In the west the Royalists had destroyed Waller's army at Roundway Down (13 July). Only in the north were things not quite so bad as they at first appeared. Newcastle had failed to exploit his success by marching southwards. On the contrary Lord Willoughby by surprising Gainsborough had severed the Royalists' communications with Newark.

Cromwell now struck a blow with an attack on Burghley House, near Stamford. The place fell after a feeble resistance (24 July), not more than six men being killed on both sides.

Meanwhile, Willoughby at Gainsborough was hard pressed by Cavendish, and Meldrum, with Cromwell's men and some Lincolnshire troops, marched to his relief. The Parliamentarians numbered some 1,200 mounted men; nineteen or twenty troops of horse and three or four companies of dragoons. Meeting at North Scarle they marched without delay (29 July). Cavendish's 'Forlorn Hope' was encountered north of the river Lea, and Cromwell relates how the Parliamentarians gradually drove them back to the summit of a steep

10 COLONEL NATHANIEL FIENNES

Wearing the dress of a cavalry officer. The armour is painted black to prevent rust, the left (or
bridle) arm is protected by a guard, and the lobster-tailed helmet is shown

From the portrait by Mirevelt

11 GENERAL JOHN LAMBERT
From a contemporary engraving

12 RICHARD CROMWELL
*Detail from a contemporary
portrait*

hill, where they were drawn up on a front of three regiments, with Cavendish's own regiment, a very strong one, in reserve. The Lincolnshire horse, under Captain Edward Ayscoghe, were supported by Meldrum with the main body, five troops from Nottingham and Northampton. Cromwell brought up the rear with his own regiment, now six or seven troops. The ground was broken up by rabbit warrens, which hindered the deployment of the Parliamentarians.

Cromwell tells us how the main body of the Royalists came on before the Roundheads were ready, and were within musket-shot when they came to the 'pitch of the hill'. He goes on:

> We endeavoured to put our men into as good order as we could, the enemy in the meantime advancing towards us, to take us at disadvantage; but in such order as we were, we charged their great body, I having the right wing. We came up horse to horse, where we disputed it with our swords and pistols a pretty time, all keeping close order, so that one could not break the other. At last, they a little shrinking, our men perceiving it, pressed in upon them, and immediately routed this whole body, some flying on one side, others on the other of the enemy's reserve; and our men, pursuing them, *had chase and execution about five or six miles.*[1]

He goes on to tell how, seeing that the reserve still stood unbroken, he kept back three troops of his regiment and got them into a body. Four of the Lincoln troops faced Cavendish's other flank, all the rest of the Roundheads being engaged in the chase.

When at last Cavendish decided to charge the Lincolners, he routed them.

> I immediately fell on his rear ... which did so astonish him, that he gave over the chase, and would fain have delivered himself from me, but I pressing on forced them down an hill, having good execution of them, and below the hill, drove the General with some of his soldiers into a quagmire, where my captain-lieutenant [James Berry] slew him with a thrust under his short ribs. The rest of the body was wholly routed, not one man staying upon the place.

In short the Parliamentarians had won a complete victory. The Lincolnshire troops had certainly done well, but the chief credit must go to Cromwell.

[1] Author's italics.

The Parliamentarians were now able to relieve Gainsborough with powder and provisions, but the day's fighting was not done. A new enemy was reported a mile away. Reinforced by about 400 of Lord Willoughby's foot, the Parliamentary force marched out to meet them. Cromwell had a quick success, routing two troops near a mill, then pushing on to the top of a near-by hill, he found himself looking down on Newcastle's whole army on the march to besiege Gainsborough. No fewer than fifty infantry colours could be seen, and a great body of horse 'which, coming so unexpectedly, put us to new consultations'.

'The foot did retire disorderly into the town . . . upon whom the enemy's horse did some small execution.' The cavalry also retired in some disorder until, after about half a mile, they came to the end of a field where Colonel Cromwell, Whalley, and Ayscoghe, rallied a body of them and faced the Cavaliers, staying their pursuit. Cromwell had only eight troops, while the Royalists were increasing rapidly as fresh squadrons rode up from the main body.

> But such was the goodness of God, giving courage and valour to our men and officers, that whilst Major Whalley and Captain Ayscoghe, sometimes the one . . . faced the enemy, sometimes the other, to the exceeding Glory of God be it spoken, and the great honour of those two gentlemen, [they] with this handful faced the enemy so and dared them to their teeth in at least eight or nine several removes.

Though their horses were exceedingly tired, they drew off in good order with the Cavaliers following up 'near carbine shot' in rear, firing at them. Cromwell rallied the main body to support the two rearguard squadrons, and asserts that he brought off his force 'without the loss of two men'.

Under the most adverse circumstances, Cromwell had carried out the intricate manœuvre of retiring by alternate squadrons. It is evident that some of the Parliamentarian troops, including apparently two or three belonging to Cromwell's own regiment, were as yet inadequately trained, but for all that Gainsborough was a great achievement. And since Meldrum's name vanishes from the story after the first paragraph, there is no question that it was Cromwell's victory. It was a great day for him. A year before he had never heard a shot fired in war. Now he had proved himself thoroughly capable of commanding a cavalry regiment in the field. But even without this success he was coming to the fore. That same day, as it chanced, he was appointed by the House of Commons to be governor of the Isle of Ely, where his home lay. A fortnight later he was named (10 August 1643) as one of the four colonels of horse in the new army to be raised by the Earl of Manchester.

But Gainsborough had not turned the tide. On 30 July Lord Willoughby surrendered that town, and it was not long before he abandoned Lincoln also, actions for which Cromwell was later to censure him. In a letter of 5 August Willoughby wrote that this set-back had 'deaded' the hearts of his men so that most of them had run away. Cromwell forwarded this letter, endorsed 'haste, haste, post-haste', to the Deputy-Lieutenants of Essex who, once more, in a time of crisis, had fallen far short of his expectations.

> Gentlemen, you see by this enclosed, the necessity of going out of our old pace. You sent indeed your part of the 2,000 foot, but when they came, they as soon returned.
>
> Is this the way to save a Kingdom? . . . Haste what you can; not your part only of 2,000 foot but I hope 2,000 foot at least. Lord Newcastle will advance into your bowels. Better join when others will join and can join with you, than stay till all be lost; hasten to our help. . . . See your men come, and some of your gentlemen and ministers come along with them, that so they may be delivered over to those shall command them; otherwise they will return at pleasure.

Cromwell had divined Newcastle's true strategy, but the Marquis was to come no nearer to the bowels of Essex, for on 2 September he sat down before Hull.

Manchester was now able to undertake the siege of Lynn, which fell on 16 September, while Cromwell and the cavalry went to assist Willoughby in Lincolnshire. Sir Thomas Fairfax and his cavalry crossed the Humber and joined Manchester, enabling him to take the field with at least 1,500 horse and perhaps 6,000 foot, and to threaten Bolingbroke Castle, seven miles south-east of Horncastle.

Newcastle ordered Sir William Widdrington, who was now the senior Royalist commander in Lincolnshire, to relieve the Castle, and by drawing on various garrisons he assembled a small force of 1,500–2,000 horse and 800 dragoons at Lincoln.

By noon on 11 October Manchester had concentrated his army on Bolingbroke Hill, where he held a council of war, the question being whether to accept battle or not. Cromwell advised against it: not only were his horses wearied by hard service, but his men were in grave want, lacking clothes, boots, and money to refurbish their arms and shoe their horses. He complained bitterly that many who could plunder and pillage felt no want, but his men, though sometimes called Anabaptists, were 'the freest from unjust practices of any in England'. Manchester was for fighting and, supported by Fairfax, had his way. Perhaps Cromwell over-rated Widdrington's Cavaliers who were outnumbered by three to one.

The two armies met near the little village of Winceby. Reaching the crest 500 yards beyond that place, the Parliamentarians could see their enemy deploying on the next ridge, about 600 yards away. As at Grantham, neither army seems to have been willing to make the first move, but at length some Royalist dragoons advanced across the dip between them. Colonel Vermuyden charged, and the Cavalier horse moved out to meet him. Thereupon Cromwell, riding well in front of his men, led out two regiments, at a good round trot, to support Vermuyden's Forlorn Hope, and the fight was on. The Roundheads rode into battle singing Psalms. Cromwell himself fell upon the Royalists immediately after their dragoons had given him their first volley, yet they were so quick reloading that they got in another when he was within half pistol shot. This killed his horse, which fell down upon him, and, as he rose up, he was knocked down again by Sir Ingram Hopton, who was killed immediately afterwards. Later 'he recovered a poor horse in a soldier's hands, and bravely mounted himself again'. This first charge was 'home-given', and performed with admirable resolution.

A second charge, led by Sir Thomas Fairfax, swept the Cavaliers from the field in the greatest disorder. The battle was a small one, but the victory was not unimportant. The Royalists now lost Gainsborough and Lincoln; Newark itself was hemmed in. Cromwell had played his part, but as he was put out of action early on, he was eclipsed on this occasion by Fairfax, whom Manchester praised with great warmth. The Earl described Cromwell as having 'behaved with honour', and there is no evidence that the latter considered this tribute less than generous. Indeed, for the first few months of their service together they got on well if only because, as Baillie puts it: 'Manchester himself, a sweet, meek man, permitted his Lieutenant-General, Cromwell, to guide all the army at his pleasure.'

6 IRONSIDES: LT.-GENERAL CROMWELL AND MARSTON MOOR

God made them as stubble to our swords . . .

No military operations disturbed the quiet of the Eastern Association during the winter months, but nevertheless, the war was approaching a crisis.

On 8 December John Pym died. To the Parliamentarians his loss seemed irreparable, while the Royalists rejoiced at his passing. That subtle diplomat, Sir Henry Vane the younger, and Cromwell's friend, Oliver St. John, now led the war party in the Commons. Vane it was that concluded the Solemn League and Covenant which in January 1644 brought the Presbyterian Scots into the war on the side of Parliament. It is no exaggeration to say that without this 'foreign intervention' the Cavaliers might well have won the First Civil War. Vane had the cunning to insert, in the Covenant to reform religion, the innocent-seeming words 'according to the word of God'. This made it possible for Cromwell and the Independents, who held with Milton that 'new presbyter is but old priest writ large', to continue to fight the battles of the Lord—battles not all of which were fought in the field. Tolerant though he may have become as Protector, Cromwell was very active at this earlier period in persecuting the Anglicans.

At Ely, Canon Hitch had had the courage to continue the choir-service. On 10 January Cromwell, as governor, wrote to him: 'Lest the soldiers should in any tumultuary or disorderly way attempt the reformation of your Cathedral Church, I require you to forbear altogether your choir-service, so unedifying and offensive; . . .'

Since Hitch ignored his threats, Cromwell with his hat on, entered the church during divine service at the head of a party of soldiers and 'attended by the rabble'. 'I am a man under authority and am commanded to dismiss this assembly', he cried. Hitch paused, but when Oliver and his followers went on up towards the communion-table, continued the service. Thereupon Cromwell returned in a passion, laid his hand on his sword, and bade the canon 'leave off his fooling and come down'. He then drove out the congregation. Incidents of this sort did more than anything to make Cromwell's name detested by the Episcopalians who made up the greater part of the Royalist party.

By the time of the Oxford Parliament, whose sessions began this same month, Cromwell was already recognized by the Royalists as one of their more relentless enemies. It was at this time that the far-sighted and worldly prelate John Williams, Archbishop of York, gave Charles advice, which though somewhat malicious was not lacking in discernment.

Cromwell, he said, 'was the most dangerous enemy his Majesty had. For tho' he were at that time of mean rank and use among them, yet he would climb higher'. Williams, when Bishop of Lincoln, had known Cromwell before 1637, 'but never knew his religion. He was a common spokesman for sectaries, and maintained their part with stubbornness. He never discoursed as if he were pleased with your Majesty, and your great officers; and indeed he loves none, that are more than his equals'. Williams ended: 'My humble motion is, that either you would win him to you by promises of fair treatment, or catch him by some stratagem, and cut him short.'

In the latter part of January Cromwell was in London and on 22 January, which seems to have been the date of his promotion to Lieutenant-General, he made a speech in the Commons. He desired that Lord Willoughby of Parham, who had commanded in Lincolnshire, might be ordered to stay in London . . . and that Manchester might be made serjeant-major-general of the associated counties. He accused Willoughby of quitting Gainsborough, when he, himself, was not too far off to have relieved him. Later he had abandoned Lincoln, leaving ammunition and arms there, and seven great pieces of ordnance. Worse, he had 'very loose and profane commanders under him'. One of these, Sir Christopher Wray, also happened to be M.P. for Grimsby, and was incensed at hearing Cromwell 'cast dirt' on Willoughby, 'who had so well deserved', and had 'much ado to have patience to hear this out to the end'. Nevertheless, after a long debate Manchester was given the appointment that Cromwell proposed.

Cromwell evidently thought well of Manchester at this time, but he soon fell foul of the major-general of the Eastern Association. This was Lawrence Crauford, a Presbyterian Scot of the most uncompromising sort, who had seen service under Gustavus Adolphus, and was a brave and efficient officer. On 10 March we find Cromwell writing to Crauford in his most downright manner, condemning the latter's decision to dismiss his lieutenant-colonel.

> Surely you are not well advised thus to turn off one so faithful to the Cause, and so able to serve you. . . . Give me leave to tell you I cannot be of your judgment that if a man notorious for wickedness, for oaths, for drinking, hath as great a share in your affection as one that fears an oath, that fears to sin, that this doth commend your election of men to serve as fit instruments in this work.
>
> Ay, but the man is an Anabaptist. Are you sure of that? Admit he be, shall that render him incapable to serve the public? He is indiscreet. It may be so, in some things, we have all human infirmities. I tell you, if you had none but such indiscreet men about you, and would be pleased to use them kindly, you would find [them] as good a fence to you as any you have yet chosen.
>
> Sir, the State, in choosing men to serve them, takes no notice of their opinions, if they be willing faithfully to serve them, that satisfies.

Nothing could seem more reasonable to the twentieth-century mind than this spirited defence of an officer whose religious views were his only crime, but Cromwell's modern biographers have omitted to point out that he himself was not above ousting an officer for the very same reason. Indeed it seems that in 1644 there was war to the knife between Independent and Presbyterian in the army of Manchester.

Crauford tells us that:

> Cromwell and his creatures did nothing but foment sedition and dissension in my Lord's army of horse, . . . to withdraw the hearts of people from the Earl of Manchester, by some sinister and pernicious course he framed a petition which was managed by Lieutenant-Colonel Whaley and Lieutenant-Colonel Lilburne.

The object of this was to put out of the army all officers who were 'not Brownists, or of such like sects'. This the Presbyterians considered 'highly mutinous' and 'much diminishing my Lord's honour and the rest of the gentlemen of the army'. At least six officers refused to sign, though they were warned that 'Cromwell did take an account who had not underwritten it, much vilifying them that did not'. One of these, Captain Armiger of Fleetwood's regiment, was 'outed' while on leave in London, and his troop given to a notorious Independent. This Cromwell did, according to Crauford, to show his power in the army. There is no doubt that by now his influence was very great. Not one of the other five who had earned his enmity was to obtain a command in the New Model Army.[1]

In March 1644 Cromwell suffered a heavy blow. His son, Captain Oliver, 'a civil young gentleman and the joy of his father', died of smallpox at Newport Pagnell.

In the same month old Meldrum, without the assistance of the Eastern Association, laid siege to Newark. On 21 March Rupert fell upon him like a thunderbolt and forced him to surrender. Cromwell, who was at Cambridge when the news arrived that Rupert was on the move, remained inactive. An anonymous opponent alleges:

> I spake to him thus: Sir, if you would march up to Newark with but 1,500 of your horse you would spoil Prince Rupert's market. He said again there is Sir John Meldrum and the rest would take the town for all the Prince; I said to him again it was as cheap for our horse to march as to lie still in the stables; whereupon he was angry and bid me hold my tongue.

Cambridge is 79 miles from Newark and we cannot be certain whether Cromwell could have arrived in time, yet Rupert, coming from Shrewsbury had over 100 miles to cover. To attempt nothing in this crisis was probably an error of judgment.

Meanwhile the Scots pressed steadily southwards. On 22 April the Earl of Leven and Lord Fairfax laid siege to York, which was held by Newcastle and a garrison of some 5,000 men.

Manchester eventually took the field and stormed Lincoln on 6 May. We know nothing of Cromwell's part in this operation,

[1] They were: Major Thomas Wilde and Captain Samuel Moody of Vermuyden's Regiment; Captain William (?) Patterson; Captain John Moody and Captain Richard Le Hunt of Fleetwood's regiment.

though the cathedral suffered from what *Mercurius Aulicus* describes as 'Cromwell's barbarous crew of Brownists': who besides destroying 'all the brave carved works there', and the monuments, 'filled each corner of that holy place with their own and horses dung, in so horrid a measure as the Lord Kimbolton [Manchester] would turn away his groom that should suffer his worst stable to lie half so nasty as he and Cromwell have made the House of God'. Wanton damage of this sort certainly made the possibility of any future settlement between Anglican Cavalier and Independent more remote.

Manchester now moved up to join in the siege of York. The fate of the north hung in the balance, but Rupert, advancing to its relief, was at Knaresborough, 18 miles due west of York, on 30 June. The Allies concentrated on 1 July on Marston Moor, six miles west of York, expecting him to advance by the most direct route. But the main body of the Cavaliers did not appear. While amusing his enemy with his advanced guard the Prince was marching rapidly round via Boroughbridge, Thornton Bridge and Poppleton to join hands with Newcastle in York. Marching 20 miles in the day, he completely outwitted his opponents—a brilliant manœuvre.

The Allied commanders now resolved to march south-west towards Cawood and Tadcaster, hoping to cut off supplies from the East and West Ridings and force Rupert to fight. The Prince, however, was eager for battle, and though outnumbered by three to two, his men came pouring out of York next day (2 July). Some of the Allies had almost reached Tadcaster before Leven heard the news, and gave orders to march back to Marston Moor, where he took up a position between the villages of Long Marston and Tockwith. The moor was open and fairly flat, though there was a ditch between the two armies.

The Allies had a large body of cavalry on their right under Sir Thomas Fairfax. Then came Baillie's Scots infantry; next, in the centre, stood Lord Fairfax's foot, and next the infantry of the Eastern Association under Crauford. Cromwell himself commanded the cavalry on the left. Besides the men of the Eastern Association he had some Scots cavalry under David Leslie to support him and some of their dragoons on his left flank.

As the summer day wore on he could see the Cavaliers marshalling their host not much more than a quarter of a mile away—one minute's gallop. Opposite him were cavalry under Byron and Urry, considerably less numerous than his own, but with two regiments of foot posted in the ditch to their front. Prince Rupert's bluecoats, their black colours conspicuous at the head of the pikemen, was one of them. These men would be able to pour a heavy fire into the Parliamentarian horse as they advanced, causing casualties and confusion before the two bodies came to blows. Rupert endeavoured to offset the disparity of numbers by supporting most of his cavalry squadrons with bodies of 200 musketeers.

For most of the day the main body of the Royalists had but a thin front opposite Crauford, but as the afternoon drew on seven great bodies of Newcastle's famous Whitecoats came up and ranged themselves checker-wise in a second and a third line. The left of the Royalist foot consisted of Rupert's men under his Major-General, Tillier, whose veteran Anglo-Irish Greencoats were prominent in the first line. A brigade of horse was drawn up behind the foot as a reserve, and here too was Rupert's 'command post'. Fairfax was opposed by Goring with the cavalry of Newcastle's army. Thus Cavalier and Roundhead set to partners on this fateful day, 17,500 Cavaliers facing the 27,000 men the Allies could muster.

It is said that during the afternoon a prisoner was brought to Rupert who asked: 'Is Cromwell there?'

While the Royalists were forming up the Allied generals watched them narrowly. Along towards evening it became clear that Rupert did not intend to attack that day; then no doubt, Fairfax, Leven and Manchester held council and determined to strike a blow themselves. There is little question that the younger Fairfax and Cromwell said their say. About 7 p.m. Rupert sat down to an al fresco supper, while the stately Marquis retired to his coach to smoke a pipe.

Suddenly, a cannon was fired from the Allied centre, and at that signal the Allied line surged forward with cries of 'God and Religion!' Hastily the Royalists dressed their ranks to receive them. Just as the armies were joining battle 'it pleased the Lord ... that a sudden and mighty great storm of rain and hail, and terrible claps of thunder were heard and seen from the clouds; as if heaven had resolved to second the assault with a fierce alarm from above'.

Over on the Roundhead right Sir Thomas Fairfax received a volley, struggled on across the ditch, and found his ranks somewhat disordered among the gorse bushes beyond. The regiment he led charged successfully, but Goring's Cavaliers struck back hard, and shouting their field-word 'God and the King!' drove the Parliament men from the field. In their flight Fairfax's troops carried away many of the Scots foot. Sir Charles Lucas, who led Goring's second line, had his men well in hand: instead of pursuing the fugitives, he wheeled and crashed into the flank of the Roundhead foot. Panic reigned: it spread along the line until Manchester himself was swept from the field. Lord Fairfax galloped home to Cawood and was seen no more that day. In the words of Chaplain Ashe 'in all appearance the day was lost', but like rocks in a boiling sea, six of the Scottish regiments stood firm amidst Goring's horse.

Meanwhile Cromwell had led his men over the ditch and on to the flat moor beyond, where they were met by Byron's front line which rode out to meet him, masking the fire of their own musketeers. The onset swept away two Royalist brigades, but ere long Oliver himself was slightly wounded in the neck. Nobody knows exactly how he came by this hurt, but family tradition says that Colonel Marcus Trevor wounded him. It is significant that Trevor's regiment was drawn up in Byron's front line precisely opposite the post that Cromwell, as Lieutenant-General, should have occupied.[1]

The fight raged hotly for a time and Cromwell's men 'had a hard pull of it; for they were charged by Rupert's bravest men both in front and flank'. Rupert discovered with remarkable speed that while all was going well on the left, the reserve was badly needed on his right. As he led it there he was met by men of his own regiment of horse from Byron's *second* line. 'Swounds! Do you run? Follow me!' he cried, and falling on Cromwell's now leaderless troopers, drove them back up the hill. But the Allies still had a shot in their locker —David Leslie's Scots, who now counter-attacked in their turn.

Meanwhile Cromwell, though wounded, had rallied a considerable part of his cavalry. The fiery Crauford, seeing these squadrons standing idle, rode up and not noticing Oliver, cursed them for poltroons. Cromwell said that he had been wounded; and Crauford apologized. Handing over the command to Crauford, Oliver rode to Tockwith to get his wound dressed.

[1] Another story is that Cromwell was wounded by one of his troopers who accidentally discharged his pistol. This is possible, but one would imagine that the Ironsides were better trained than that.

The battle raged on, the Royalists fighting stubbornly, 'coming to a close fight with the sword, and standing like an iron wall, so that they were not easily broken . . .' But broken they were at last. By this time Cromwell was once more at the head of his men. Leaving Leslie to pursue the remnants of Rupert's right, he prepared for further service. Before he had determined what to do Sir Thomas Fairfax appeared. He had cut his way free of Goring's men, and though slashed across the cheek, had ridden round the rear of the Royalist army. The two generals held a hurried consultation in the gathering dusk, and then, following the route by which Fairfax had come, fell upon Goring's now scattered regiments. This relieved the pressure on Baillie's infantry whose hedgehogs of pikemen were still holding out.

The Allied infantry, such as were left, now began to advance, while Newcastle's Whitecoats fell back into White Syke Close, where they fought it out almost to the last man. Night had fallen long since, but the fight went on by the light of a harvest moon. When the end came, most of the Royalist foot were shattered beyond all hope of reorganization; twenty guns had been taken. The cavalry too, had suffered severely. Lucas and Tillier were prisoners; Newcastle gave up the struggle and fled to Hamburg. Leaving Sir Thomas Glemham to defend York as best he could, Rupert gathered up the remnants of his cavalry, perhaps 6,000 in all, and made his way back into Lancashire.

Unhappily we have no full despatch from Cromwell's pen, though a letter to his friend Colonel Valentine Walton gives some details:

> Truly England and the Church of God hath had a great favour from the Lord, in this great victory given unto us, such as the like never was since this war began. [It was obtained, he goes on], by the Lord's blessing upon the godly party principally. We never charged but we routed the enemy. The left wing, which I commanded, being our own horse, saving a few Scots in our rear, beat all the Prince's horse. God made them as stubble to our swords, we charged their regiments of foot with our horse, routed all we charged.
>
> Sir, God hath taken away your eldest son by a cannon-shot. It brake his leg. We were necessitated to have it cut off, whereof he died.
>
> Sir, you know my trials this way;[1] but the Lord supported me with

---

[1] The recent death of Captain Oliver Cromwell.

this: that the Lord took him into the happiness we all pant after and live for. There is your precious child full of glory, not to know sin nor sorrow any more. He was a gallant young man, exceeding gracious. God give you His comfort. Before his death he was so full of comfort that . . . he could not express it, it was so great above his pain. This he said unto us. Indeed it was admirable.

Marston Moor was the hardest fought fight of all the war—'a damned near run thing'. 'I am sure', Rupert is reported to have said, 'my men fought well, and therefore know no reason of our rout but this, because the devil did help his servants'. The casualties may have been as many as 4,000 killed—nearly ten per cent of those engaged, which considering the inefficient firearms of the day is fairly heavy. Cromwell's reputation now stood very high with both friend and foe. 'Major-General Leslie seeing us thus pluck a victory out of the enemies' hands, professed Europe had no better soldiers', says Manchester's Scoutmaster-General, while Rupert dubbed him 'Ironsides' —a name soon to be given to his men as well.

The Allies, though outnumbering the Cavaliers had been within an ace of defeat—and a defeat would have been decisive, for the Scots would have gone home. Without Cromwell and his Ironsides the cause of Parliament must have been lost irretrievably on the field of Marston Moor.

7 SECOND NEWBURY AND THE SELF-DENYING ORDINANCE

. . . that darling of the sectaries . . .

FROM the point of view of national strategy the Parliamentarians did little enough to exploit their great victory at Marston Moor. Leven went north to lay siege to Newcastle; Fairfax occupied himself with reducing the Royalist fortresses in Yorkshire while Manchester marched back into the Eastern Association, which he had formed and which he felt bound to protect. In the south the Parliamentarians had failed to combine against 'the Oxford Army' with the result that Waller suffered a sharp reverse at Cropredy Bridge (29 June) and Essex's foot and artillery were forced to surrender at Lostwithiel (2 September). They were now compelled to concentrate, and by the end of October an army, built up from those of Manchester, Waller and Essex, with a brigade of the London Trained Bands, faced the King north of Newbury.

The old friendly relations between Cromwell and his general did not survive this period. Contempt for Manchester's parochial attitude towards the conduct of war was part of the trouble; distrust of the Presbyterians was even more important. 'I will not deny', Cromwell said, 'but that I desire to have none in my army but such as are of the Independent judgment', adding, 'that in case there should be propositions for peace, . . . such as might not stand with the ends that honest men should aim at, this army might prevent such a mischief.' A kind of inverted snobbery also embittered their relationship. The Earl alleged that Cromwell hoped to 'live to see never a nobleman in England, . . . it would not be well until Manchester was but Mr. Montague'.

As for the Scots Cromwell had told his general:

> In the way they now carry themselves, pressing for their [church] discipline, I could as soon draw my sword against them as against any in the King's army.

Cromwell began to show his dissatisfaction openly in a letter of 5 September to his friend Colonel Walton in which he voices his 'grief of heart' over the sad condition of affairs in the West.

> We have some amongst us much slow in action: if we could all intend our own ends less, and our ease too, our business in this Army would go on wheels for expedition.

It was now Manchester's clear duty to place his army between the King and London, a course which Cromwell urged on him two days running (6 and 7 September). The Earl, no strategist, merely became exasperated and threatened to hang anyone who attempted to advise him further. Cromwell asserted that Crauford was at the bottom of the trouble, and told the Earl that his colonels would resign in a body unless a new major-general was appointed. Unable to reconcile their difference, all three generals repaired to London and laid their dispute before the Committee of Both Kingdoms. A compromise was reached. Crauford was to retain his command, but the army of the Eastern Association was to march to the aid of the army in the West. No doubt Cromwell thought this a small price to pay for the acceptance of a sound strategy.

The quarrel had been the occasion for Cromwell to visit London and take his place in the House for the first time in seven months. On 13 September there was an important debate marking a stage in the religious struggle between Presbyterian and Independent, and this he was able to attend. The question concerned the form of ordination for the proposed church when government by bishops and archbishops should have been abolished. St. John, prompted by Cromwell, proposed a motion on the queston 'how far tender consciences, who cannot in all things submit to the common rule . . . may be borne with according to the word. . . .' This was accepted without a division, and before the close of the sitting, the Speaker, Lenthall, by command of the House, gave thanks to Lieutenant-General Cromwell for his fidelity in the cause in hand, and in particular for his faithful service at Marston Moor 'where God made him a special instrument in obtaining that great victory'. For the moment the Independents were in the ascendant.

On 14 September Cromwell took the oath of secrecy as a member of the Committee of Both Kingdoms and three days later returned to his military duties.

★   ★   ★

On the evening of 26 October the combined Parliamentarian armies, 17,500 strong, were concentrated at Thatcham, three miles east of Newbury. The King could muster only 9,000 men in his position north of that town, but the ground favoured the Cavaliers. They were in a rough triangle with a strongpoint at each angle—Shaw House, Donnington Castle and Speen Hill—and with the river Kennet guarding them to the southwards. Their general reserve was in the Speenhamland area. It was a formidable position laid out rather in the style of World War II with all-round defence and defence in depth.

To tackle it the Parliamentarians adopted an ambitious plan which would make use of their superior forces. Waller, with some 13,000 men, was to make a wide detour round the north of the Royalist position and come in on Speen from the west, while Manchester with about 4,500 was to attack Shaw House as soon as battle was joined. The gunfire from the west would be the signal for his onset. Cromwell's horse were part of Waller's command.

For their plan to succeed two things were essential: first, that the flank march should be a complete surprise to the Royalists; second, that the attacks by Waller and Manchester should be practically simultaneous. A measure of surprise was gained, for as the day wore on many of the Cavaliers went off foraging, but Manchester's attack did not go in until about an hour after the assault on Speen.

The battle began about three o'clock in the afternoon. Skippon, who commanded Essex's foot, advanced with Balfour's cavalry on his right and Cromwell's on his left, stormed the Royalist earthwork west of Speen, took nine guns, pushed the Royalists out of the village, and fought his way forward as far as the next hedge bordering Speenhamland before he was held up. About four o'clock Balfour advanced between Speen Hill and the river Kennet and got into Speenhamland, where the King was, but was repulsed by part of the Royalist reserve of cavalry.

The fate of the kingdom now hung in the balance. For a space it was well-nigh impossible that the Royalist army should escape irretrievable disaster. At the same time as Balfour attacked, Cromwell at the head of the cavalry of the Eastern Association, which cannot have numbered less than 1,500 men, advanced, between Speen Hill and Donnington Castle, making for the north side of the great field. The Royalists were bound to launch a large part of their reserve against Balfour. If, therefore, Cromwell could now deploy in the open field, crumpling up the western flank of the King's position, escape for the Royalists would be impossible. But now it fell to that wayward genius George Goring, who with all his faults was a great man in an emergency, to prolong the war by another year.

Sir Edward Walker gives the clearest account of this phase of the battle. He tells us how before Cromwell's men had reached the great field General Goring put himself into the head of the Earl of Cleveland's brigade—about 800 strong—and fell upon them, and forced them back in great confusion, and then got over the hedge, where he was again charged by another body, but he quickly defeated them also. . . . This charge was the more gallant, because this brigade of horse, not only went over the ditch to meet the rebels, but passed by three bodies of the rebels foot, who shot at them both when they pursued . . . and as they came back.

In short, Cromwell made even less progress than Balfour and, although he had Skippon's left wing to support him, was driven back by a force which he must have outnumbered by at least two to one.

The Ironsides had now shot their bolt, and according to Crauford, all Cromwell's horse 'stood still while Colonel Henry Barclay's brigade was charged three times'. When Lieutenant-General John Middleton 'seeing so great absurdities and oversights', came and desired Cromwell to charge he refused. Middleton now charged with one squadron, but was routed by the Cavaliers, and being unsupported, had to fly for his life. The upshot was that 'there was no service performed at all by Cromwell'. It is not difficult to imagine an indignant Middleton pouring the tale of his narrow escape into the willing ears of his fellow Scot, Crauford.

Cromwell himself has left no account of this phase of the battle though in a narrative describing Manchester's short-comings he says that about half an hour after sunset (about 5 p.m.) he and his fellow commanders on the Speen flank 'did cease and draw our men together to avoid confusion in the dark by that scattered way of fighting'; nevertheless, the firing continued until about nine o'clock at night. Meanwhile Manchester's assault on Shaw House had been beaten off with the loss of two guns and many men.

Although the Parliamentarians had been repulsed at all points, considerable confusion reigned among the Cavaliers, particularly the Western army. The King retreated that night, leaving his Train of Artillery under the works of Donnington Castle.

Oliver's part in this battle has caused much comment both then and now. Crauford's opinion, based on 'the report of the best there', was that 'if Cromwell had played the part that became him, the enemy had been totally routed'. We know that at this period he was discontented with the way the Parliamentarians were conducting the war, and this may account for any inertia at Second Newbury. Mr. Ashley, among modern historians, takes the view that Cromwell's lack of progress is sufficiently accounted for by the fact that the ground was unfavourable. 'Cromwell's cavalry found itself on most unfavourable ground, intersected with hedges and coming under cannon fire from Donnington.' But is this really an adequate explanation? There were only four guns in Donnington Castle and presumably they were not all pointing southwards. Their rate of fire cannot possibly have been more than one round in three minutes, even at the crisis of a battle. They were, moreover, about 1,000 yards away, rather beyond the best range for the field-guns of the day. The hedges may have been very difficult, if so the ground must have changed a great deal, which is not impossible. But the really significant point is, of course, that despite the fire of Skippon's musketeers, Goring managed to get across the hedge. If he could do it, why did Oliver fail?

But is it not being too subtle to look for any sinister reason for this failure? After all, Crauford, though a man of honour, detested Cromwell and was not himself an eyewitness. Perhaps the simplest explanation is the best: that Goring made a brilliant charge and succeeded where so many had failed in beating Cromwell and his Ironsides.

★   ★   ★

The Parliamentarians lingered about Newbury and made little attempt at pursuit. In consequence the King was able to recover his artillery from Donnington Castle (9 November). The Royalists offered battle, but the Parliamentarian Council of War declined to fight.

Manchester put forward political as well as military reasons against risking battle:

'If we beat the King ninety-nine times, yet he is King still, and so will his posterity be after him but if the King beat us once we shall all be hanged, and our posterity made slaves.'

'My Lord, if this be so, why did we take up arms at first?' was Cromwell's unanswerable retort. 'This is against fighting ever hereafter. If so, let us make peace, be it ever so base.'

The armies now went into winter quarters, and the Parliamentarian generals repaired to London to air their many grievances in their respective Houses. When on 25 November Cromwell took his place in the Commons, he had to listen to a motion very unpleasing in his ears: a request to the Lords 'to consider of bringing up the Scottish army southwards', to form a nucleus round which the broken English armies could reform. This was the last thing Oliver wanted. His aim had long been to build up an English army which could act independently of Scots and Presbyterians. Waller now rose and made a speech in which apparently he complained that Manchester had failed to march to his aid early in October. Cromwell followed, describing the Newbury campaign in acrimonious detail, and charging Manchester with a desire to bring the war to an end on terms since 'it might be disadvantageous to bring the King too low'.

The affair was referred to a committee under the chairmanship of Zouch Tate. Manchester, sweet, meek man though he was, counter-attacked, describing Cromwell as 'a factious and somewhat inert officer'. He himself had always conformed to the resolutions of the Council of War and pointed out that Cromwell acknowledged this. His Lieutenant-General despised the nobility and had described the Assembly of Divines as persecutors. Worse still he wished to have none but Independents in the Army of the Eastern Association.

Cromwell denied none of this.

What had begun as a purely military quarrel had now developed into a first-class political row. The Scots in particular were out for Cromwell's blood. 'This fire was long under the embers', wrote Baillie; 'now its broken out, we trust, in a good time. It's like, for the interest of our nation, we must crave reason of that darling of the sectaries, and, in obtaining his removal from the army, which himself by his over-rashness has procured, to break the power of that potent faction.'

On 3 December a conference was held at Essex House, at which Essex and others met the Scottish Commissioners. They discussed the question whether to accuse Cromwell under a clause of the Covenant by which anyone who divided the Kingdoms from one another could be brought to justice. But Maynard, the lawyer, warned them that 'Lieutenant-General Cromwell is a person of great favour and interest with the House of Commons, and with some of the Peers likewise, and therefore there must be proofs, . . . to prevail with the Parliament to adjudge him to be an incendiary'.

Cromwell soon got wind of these proceedings and next day (4 December) he made a long speech in which he absolutely denied all charges against himself, and made another severe attack on Manchester. He now had the House on his side, but the whole affair was taking on the nature of a struggle with the Lords and might well do disastrous damage to the cause. In this crisis Cromwell changed his tack, and revealed for the first time more than ordinary political skill. When, on 9 December, Zouch Tate presented the report of his committee Cromwell rose, and abandoning the personal quarrel with Manchester, exposed for all to see the fundamental errors of the system on which the Parliamentarians had so far conducted the war.

> It is now the time to speak, or forever hold the tongue. The important occasion now is no less than to save a nation out of a bleeding, nay almost dying, condition, . . . casting off all lingering proceedings, like those of soldiers of fortune beyond the sea, to spin out a war . . .

Men on both sides were saying

> the Members of both Houses have got great places and commands, and the sword into their hands; and, . . . will perpetually continue themselves in grandeur, and not permit the War speedily to end, lest their own power should determine with it. . . . I know the worth of those commanders, Members of both Houses, who are yet in power. But, if I may speak my conscience without reflection upon any, I do conceive if the Army be not put into another method, and the War more vigorously prosecuted, the people can bear the War no longer, and will enforce you to a dishonourable peace.
>
> But this I would recommend to your prudence—not to insist upon any complaint or oversight of any Commander-in-Chief . . . for as I must acknowledge myself guilty of oversight, so I know they can rarely be avoided in military matters. . . . And I hope we have such true English hearts and zealous affection towards the general weal of our Mother Country as no Member of either House will scruple to deny themselves, and their own private interests, for the public good . . .

This speech deserves to be considered as one of the best and most effective Cromwell ever made, leading, as it did to the passage of the Self-Denying Ordinance and the formation of the New Model Army.

8   THE NEW MODEL

... a company of poor ignorant men ...

AFTER his defeat at Cropredy Bridge, Waller, complaining of the mutinous behaviour of the City brigade and the Essex and Hertfordshire levies, who made up the greater part of his army, had written to the Committee of Both Kingdoms saying: 'My Lords, till you have an army merely your own that you may command, it is in a manner impossible to do anything of importance.' In the New Model the Parliamentarians at last had such an army; a professional force which would go where it was told, so long as it got its pay.

The New Model consisted of: 11 regiments of horse, each 600 strong; a regiment of dragoons, 1,000 strong; and 12 regiments of foot, each 1,200 strong, a total of 22,000. Sufficient men were available to make up the cavalry: the majority came from the Eastern Association, Cromwell's double regiment of Ironsides forming the two new ones of Fairfax and Whalley. In March only 7,174 foot were available and the deficiency had to be made up by impressment.

The General of the New Model was Sir Thomas Fairfax who had won a great reputation in the north. Though a rather inarticulate man, modest and religious, he was a great leader in action.

In March 1645 Weymouth and Taunton were hard pressed by Goring, and Waller was ordered to relieve them. The New Model was not yet ready and, as Waller's own forces were insufficient, Cromwell's regiment was ordered to reinforce him. But the Ironsides did not feel inclined to go on this service and grew mutinous, so that the House was compelled to send Cromwell himself. Waller found Oliver a loyal subordinate, though, influenced perhaps by his failure at Second Newbury, he had no great opinion of his talents. Some years later he wrote:

> I cannot but mention the wonder which I have oft times had to see this eagle in his eirey; he at this time, had never shown extraordinary parts; nor do I think he did himself believe that he had them; ... As an officer he was obedient, and did never dispute my orders, nor argue upon

them. He did indeed seem to have great cunning; and whilst he was cautious of his own words . . . he made others talk, until he had, as it were sifted them, and known their most intimate designs.

The first encounter took place at Andover on 9 March. The Parliamentarians captured Lord Percy, and a small troop of some thirty Royalists. Waller, who was indisposed, desired Cromwell to entertain his prisoners. The latter discovered among them 'a youth of so fair a countenance that he doubted of his condition'. Oliver, who loved an innocent jest, 'willed him to sing, which he did with such a daintiness, that Cromwell scrupled not to say to Lord Percy that, being a warrior, he did wisely to be accompanied by Amazons. On which that lord, in some confusion, did acknowledge that she was a damsel'.

On the night of the 10th Waller and Cromwell beat up Colonel James Long's regiment in its quarters near Lavington, Wiltshire, an action in which the Ironsides behaved with all their former valour and obedience.

Waller's campaign against Goring produced no important results and on 19 April Cromwell repaired to Windsor to pay his respects to Fairfax, before retiring from the service under the Self-Denying Ordinance. But next day orders came for him from the Committee of Both Kingdoms. The New Model was still not ready, but the King seemed to be about to take the field, intending to move his Train of Artillery from Oxford to the Severn Valley. Cromwell was to take a brigade of horse into the circle of Royalist fortresses round Oxford and hinder this design.

On 23 April Oliver failed to surprise the Earl of Northampton's brigade of horse at Islip but found means to ferry his force across the Cherwell.[1] Next day, as Cromwell puts it, Northampton 'came to make an infall upon me'. Fairfax's regiment quickly took the field, and the rest 'drew out with all possible speed'. The general's troop charged a whole squadron of Cavaliers and immediately broke it. Other Roundhead troops came 'seasonably on', and the rest of the Royalists were soon put into confusion. In a pursuit of three or four miles many were killed, while 200 prisoners and about 400 horses

---

[1] According to tradition, one Beckley ferried the Ironsides across and in return Cromwell gave him perpetual fishing rights from Islip to the stretch of river where the Cherwell Hotel now stands. When Robert Graves lived at Islip, one William, alias 'Fisher' Beckley, still enjoyed this right (*Good-bye to All That*, p.398).

were taken. Many escaped towards Oxford and Woodstock, some were drowned, and others got into Bletchington House, where Colonel Francis Windebank had a garrison of about 200. Cromwell summoned him to surrender and, after a long treaty, he did so at about midnight. 'I did much doubt the storming of the house, it being strong and well manned, and I having few dragoons, and this not being my business; and yet we got it.' Windebank paid for this surrender with his life.

Moving westwards, Cromwell fell upon 300 foot at Bampton in the Bush, 18 miles west of Oxford.

> The enemy presently barricadoed up the town; got a pretty strong house. My body came up about eleven in the night, I sent them a summons. They slighted it; I put myself in a posture that they should not escape me, hoping to deal with them in the morning. My men charged them up to their barricadoes in the night, but truly they were of so good resolution that we could not force them from it, and indeed they killed some of my horses, and I was forced to wait until the morning.

Summoned again, the Royalists eventually surrendered.

So far things had gone very well, and on 29 April Cromwell, who had now reached Faringdon, decided to attack the castle. 'I will not spare a man of you, if you put me to a storm', he wrote. To this Lieutenant-Colonel Roger Burges replied stoutly: 'We would have you know you are not now at Bletchington. . . . We fear not your storming nor will have any more parleys.'

About three next morning Cromwell, who had been reinforced by 1,200 foot from the garrison of Abingdon, attempted to take the place by escalade. He attacked in three places at once, but failed everywhere. At the south-west sconce one of Whalley's captains, Henry Cannon, was the first to rear up a ladder. Burges himself thrust him into the ditch with a pike, and the Roundheads fell back, leaving their ladders against the works. The Royalists, protected by their walls, lost only six men, but in claiming to have slain 200 of their assailants they may have been using their imagination. Even so, the tone of Cromwell's letter of 30 April was altogether different to the summons that went before.

'There shall be no interruption of your viewing and gathering together the dead bodies, and I do acknowledge it as a favour, your willingness to let me dispose of them.' Thanking Burges[1] for his civility to his prisoners, he adds 'If you accept of equal exchange, I shall perform my part'.

It was an unhappy ending to an otherwise brilliant raid. The easy success at Bletchington had led Oliver to overplay his hand. His force was not capable of taking so strong a fortress by escalade, ever a most difficult operation of war. Still the raid had been a damaging blow to the Royalists. Cromwell had carried off most of the heavy draught horses in the district, seriously affecting the mobility of their artillery.

On 10 May, despite the Self-Denying Ordinance, Parliament prolonged Cromwell's period of command for forty days, and on the 28th, when the King, near Leicester, was threatening the Eastern Association, Cromwell was sent hotfoot to Ely to organize the defence. On 10 June Fairfax and his council of war petitioned Parliament to make him Lieutenant-General of the New Model.

> The general esteem and affection which he hath both with the officers and soldiers of this whole army, his own personal worth and ability for the employment, his great care, diligence, courage, and faithfulness ... constant presence and blessing of God that have accompanied him, make us look upon it as the duty we owe to you and the public, to make it our suit.

Without waiting for a reply, Fairfax sent to Cromwell at Ely, appointing him Lieutenant-General and warning him that a battle was imminent. On the 13th Cromwell rode into camp at the head of 600 horse to be welcomed 'with a mighty shout'. The news spread through the army: 'Ironsides is come to head us'. He had indeed arrived in the nick of time, for the battle of Naseby was fought next day.

A contemporary picture-map gives a very fair idea of the order in which the two armies were drawn up, but in some respects it is misleading. It gives the impression that they were evenly matched, but in fact Fairfax had about 13,000 men, while the King certainly had not more than 9,000.

Cromwell, as Lieutenant-General, had command of the cavalry on the Roundheads' right. He was opposed by Langdale with 1,600

[1] Burges later distinguished himself by his defence of Cornet Castle, Guernsey which held out until 19 December 1651.

of the Northern Horse, whom he outnumbered by at least two to one. In the centre Skippon was opposed by Astley, who, like himself, was a veteran of the Dutch service. Ireton, recently promoted Commissary-General, commanded the cavalry on the Parliamentarian left, a post for which he had scarcely sufficient experience. He was opposed by Prince Maurice.

Though he was actually to command on the right Cromwell was responsible for drawing up the whole of the cavalry. He set about his task in a mood of mystical exaltation.

> ... when I saw the enemy draw up and march in gallant order towards us, and we a company of poor ignorant men, to seek how to order our battle ... I could not (riding alone about my business) but smile out to God in praises, in assurance of victory, because God would, by things that are not, bring to naught things that are ... and God did it. O that men would therefore praise the Lord, and declare the wonders that He doth for the children of men!

An eyewitness afterwards recalled that just before the battle a fit of laughter seized Oliver.

The battle began about ten o'clock, with a general advance by the Royalist army. On the right Rupert took command, and after a hard fight broke Ireton's wing and drove most of his men back beyond the wagon-laager. In the centre Astley, suffering remarkably little damage from the musketry and artillery of the New Model, did notable execution. Sir Edward Walker could see the Parliamentarian colours falling and their foot in great disorder.

On Cromwell's wing, however, it was a very different story. He did not wait for Langdale's charge but advanced to meet him, the Ironsides shouting 'God our strength!' and the Cavaliers 'Queen Mary!' Whalley charged two divisions of the Northern Horse 'who made a very gallant resistance, and firing at a very close charge, they came to the sword'. Langdale's men were routed and fled back to Prince Rupert's Bluecoats. Thus sheltered behind their foot they rallied. The ground did not favour the advance of Cromwell's men, for there were furze bushes and rabbit warrens, which disordered them somewhat. Even so they succeeded in driving back the whole of Langdale's wing for a quarter of a mile except those who had rallied near Rupert's regiment.

Meanwhile, Fairfax had thrown in his infantry reserves and was just managing to hold Astley.

Cromwell, following up his success, used part of his wing to keep the Royalist horse from coming to the rescue of their foot, and with the rest attacked Astley's left flank. Colonel George Lisle's brigade resisted with incredible courage and resolution, although attacked in flanks, front and rear, until Fairfax called up his own regiment of foot which fell on with butt-end of muskets: the General charged them at the same time with his horse and so broke them. Charles, at the head of his reserve, was watching the scene from the slopes of Dust Hill. It was now or never. A desperate charge could still turn the day. The King and his Lifeguard were about to attempt it when the Earl of Carnwath laid hold of Charles' bridle, and turned his horse about, swearing and saying 'will you go upon your death?'

While the King and Prince Rupert were vainly endeavouring to rally their horse, Fairfax was labouring to get his army into good order again. His infantry, busy securing prisoners and completing the destruction of Astley's brigades, were now a quarter of a mile behind the cavalry. Fairfax brought them up between the two wings of horse which had already reformed, 'whereby there was framed, as it were in a trice, a second good Batalia at the latter end of the day'. The end had come—the King rode from the field and was pursued all the way to Leicester. The three hours' fight had cost him 5,000 men killed and taken, twelve guns and 200 carriages.

Cromwell gives us little detail of the fighting:

> The General served you with all faithfulness and honour; and the best commendation I can give him is, that I dare say he attributes all to God, and would rather perish than assume to himself . . . Honest men served you faithfully in this action. Sir, they are trusty; I beseech you in the name of God, not to discourage them . . . He that ventures his life for the liberty of his country, I wish he trust God for the liberty of his conscience, and you for the liberty he fights for.

Nowadays the pundits of the Staff College might well raise their eyebrows to see the second-in-command compiling the despatches and giving his general a 'mention' for his faithfulness and valour.

The Commons allowed Oliver's letter to be published, but lopped

off the last paragraph which contained so much that was unpalatable
to the Presbyterian majority. The Lords, however, exercised no such
censorship, so, in due course, the full version saw the light.

The King now had no field army, except that under Goring in the
West. For Fairfax the proper strategy was to try conclusions with
this force, before the Royalists could build it up from their various
garrisons and make head once more against the New Model. It took
the Parliamentarians some time to settle upon this plan, but on 10
July Fairfax and Goring faced each other near Langport in Somerset.
By a feint towards Taunton the Royalist general had induced Fairfax
to detach 4,000 men in that direction, so that when battle was joined
Fairfax with 10,000 did not greatly outnumber his own 7,000
men.

Langport, then a Royalist garrison, lies near the junction of the
Yeo and the Parrett. A thousand yards east is Huish Episcopi with its
splendid church. The Royalist position ran along the west of a brook,
the Wagg Rhyne, which flows down Pidsbury Bottom and crosses
the Langport-Long Sutton road about 300 yards east of the church.
The slope down to the brook is not steep at this point, but further
north it is more of an obstacle to cavalry. Royalist musketeers occupied hedges along the line of Pidsbury Bottom with cavalry in support on the ridge and two guns covering the ford or 'pass' on the
Long Sutton road. Fairfax, however, decided on a frontal attack. By
noon his guns had silenced the two Royalist pieces. Then in an hour's
fighting the Roundheads won a footing on the far side of the
Rhyne.

The decisive phase of the battle had come. Cromwell now commanded Whalley's major, Christopher Bethell, to charge with 120
horse and gain the hill. Although his men could scarcely pass two
abreast, Bethell played his part 'with the greatest gallantry imagin-
able' and broke two bodies of horse belonging to Goring's own
brigade 'at sword's point'. The Royalists counter-charged with
nearly 400 fresh cavalry, but, as Cromwell himself relates, Bethell
'set them all going, until, oppressed with multitudes, he brake
through them, . . .' Major John Desborough, once Cromwell's
quartermaster, seconded Bethell with about three troops and, driving back a great body of the Cavaliers they 'gave such an unexpected
terror to the enemy's army that set them all a running'. The

Parliamentarians now advanced, and Goring's army was pursued all the way to Bridgwater.

This was the last time the Western Army dared to face the New Model in a pitched battle. Many a Royalist stronghold still held out, but Fairfax was master of the field. He set himself to subdue the west step by step, garrison by garrison.

On 23 July Bridgwater fell. Cromwell had a narrow escape when Mrs. Wyndham, the wife of Colonel Wyndham, the Governor, fired a cannon at him from the walls, killing an officer by his side. Afterwards she sent a trumpeter to ask if he had received her 'love token', adding that if he were a courtier he would return the compliment.

Cromwell's next operation was against the Clubmen, as the peasantry of Somerset and Devon, who turned out to defend their cattle against both sides, were called. On 4 August he dispersed two parties of them. The second, which was drawn up in an old Roman fort on Hambledon Hill near Shaftesbury, showed fight—'through the animation of their leaders, and especially two vile ministers'. The Roundhead cavalry made short work of them. Cromwell's letter to Fairfax gives a plain unvarnished tale of an action which was not so much like a battle as an operation in aid of the Civil Power. He could hardly have handled the business better—using the minimum of force—and on this occasion at least he does not ascribe his success to the direct intervention of the Almighty.

The New Model now sat down before Bristol, the second city of the Kingdom. On 2 September Cromwell, along with Fairfax, Ireton, and twenty-two other officers, signed a letter to Leven and the Scots, who had been besieging Hereford. There was bad news from Scotland where 'God, for his best and secret ends' had 'been pleased to suffer' Montrose to prevail at Alford (2 July) and Kilsyth (15 August). Their 'bowels yearn towards' their Scots comrades the more because the latter's sufferings in their own kingdom were chiefly due to their assisting in England 'against the power that was risen up against the Lord himself, and his anointed ones'.

Bristol was stormed on 10 September and once more Fairfax left it to Cromwell to produce his despatch (14 September). It is printed in the *Lords Journals* with the omission of two paragraphs, and with some alterations to make it appear as if Fairfax had written it himself. The Lieutenant-General of the Horse had but little part to play in a siege and only the passage which the Lords thought fit to suppress is drawn upon here.

> . . . Presbyterians, Independents, all had here the same spirit of faith and prayer; . . . they agree here, know no names of difference: *pity it is it should be otherwise anywhere.* . . . As for being united in forms, commonly called Uniformity, every Christian will be for peace-sake study and do, *as far as conscience will permit;*[1] and from brethren, in things of the mind we look for no compulsion, but that of light and reason. In other things, God hath put the sword into the Parliament's hands, for the terror of evil-doers, and the praise of them that do well. . . . That God may maintain it in your hands, and direct you in the use thereof, is the prayer of
>
> Your humble servant,
> OLIVER CROMWELL

It must have been reasonably clear to the Lords that their humble servant had no great confidence that the Independents would get 'a square deal' when the war should be won.

★   ★   ★

In October Cromwell was sent to clear Fairfax's communications with London by reducing three Royalist garrisons in Hampshire and Wiltshire. On the 6th he reports to Lenthall the surrender of Winchester after a feeble resistance. 'You see God is not weary of doing you good: . . .'

The castle, which was well-manned and provisioned, mounted seven cannon, '. . . the works were exceedingly good and strong. It's very likely it would have cost much blood to have gained it by storm. We have not lost twelve men; this is repeated to you, that God may have all the praise, for it's all His due.'

Basing House was the next place attacked. Here the old Marquis of Winchester had twice sustained a close siege, so that the place seemed more formidable than it really was. An ancient house rebuilt and enlarged in Henry VIII's time and strengthened during the war by earthworks can hardly be regarded as more than a third-class fortress, but its position on the main road from London to Salisbury (A.30) was important, and the garrison, though only 370 strong, was full of fight. When Cromwell arrived (8 October) Colonel Dalbier had been besieging the place since August and had pushed

---

[1] Author's italics.

his approaches up almost under the defenders' works. Cromwell had in all some 7,000 men to encompass Basing, besides a formidable artillery. His five great guns included a whole cannon (63-pounder) and two demi-cannons (47-pounders). Dalbier's artillery included one or more 16-inch mortars.

After several days of bombardment the Roundheads prepared to storm the two breaches made. According to his chaplain, Hugh Peters, Cromwell spent much of the night in prayer. 'Strengthened by the text from Psalms 115.8, which was such comfort to icono- clasts, "They that make them are like unto them, so is every one that trusteth in them", he prepared to attack these idol-worshippers . . .' (Abbott).

Cromwell describes the assault which went in at daybreak of 14 October:

> I thank God, I can give you a good account of Basing. We stormed, this morning, after six of the clock. The signal for falling on was the firing four of our cannon, which being done, our men fell on with great resolution and cheerfulness. . . . Colonel Pickering stormed the new House, passed through, and got the gate of the Old House; where- upon they summoned [sounded] a parley, which our men would not hear.

Meanwhile, Colonel Edward Montague's and Sir Hardress Wal- ler's regiments assaulted the strongest work, where the Royalists kept their main guard, and beat them from it, capturing a culverin. This done they drew up their ladders after them, and swarmed over yet another work, and the wall of the house.

A Parliamentarian account says:

'The dispute was long and sharp, the enemy . . . desired no quarter, and I believe that they had but little offered them. . . . They were most of them Papists, therefore our muskets and our swords did show but little compassion.'

In the heat of the storm, which lasted about two hours, 70 to 100 of the garrison were slain, including the daughter of Doctor Griffith, 'who by her railing provoked our soldiers (then in heat) into a further passion' (Peters). Fleetwood's fanatical Major Thomas Harrison who, though a cavalryman, took part in the storm, killed two Royalist majors, the second, it seems, in cold blood. 'Cursed is he that doeth the Lord's work negligently', said he.

The soldiers soon gave over the slaughter to plunder the house, though 'eight or nine gentlewomen of rank running forth together, were entertained somewhat coarsely . . .' and others were wounded, trying to prevent the soldiers from killing their friends. The plundering went on until late at night and the spoil was prodigious. One soldier had 120 gold pieces, others plate or jewels. One got three bags of silver but being unable to keep his own counsel ended up with only half a crown. Altogether nearly 300 Royalists were taken. The stormers lost about 40 killed. The trophies included 10 guns and the Marquis's colours with the motto *Donec Pax Reddit Terris*— 'Until peace return to the earth'.

Cromwell personally is not to be blamed for the atrocities during the storm. He had summoned the place on 11 October, and the garrison by rejecting the summons had forfeited their right to quarter. Their spirit is well illustrated by the undaunted conduct of the captive Marquis himself. Peters plaguing him with arguments, he broke out: 'If the King had no more ground in England but Basing House, I would adventure as I did, and maintain it to the uttermost'.

Cromwell, who estimated that the place would need a garrison of 800, recommended that it should be slighted. He pointed out that a strong quarter at Newbury, guarding the passage of the Kennet, would prevent any incursion by the Royalist garrisons of Donnington, Wallingford or Faringdon, and would secure the trade between Bristol and London. The gentry of Sussex and Hampshire would rather 'maintain a garrison on a frontier than in their bowels'.

Cromwell next moved against Langford House in Wiltshire, which the governor, Lieutenant-Colonel Sir Bartholomew Pell, surrendered on 17 October. When the garrison marched out, six Roundhead soldiers were arrested for plundering Royalist officers contrary to the terms of surrender. Cromwell had them tried by a council of war. One was hanged and the other five were sent to Sir Thomas Glemham, the governor of Oxford, to deal with as he saw fit. Glemham, acknowledging the noble spirit behind Cromwell's action, set them free.

The New Model wintered round Exeter but took the field once more in January, concentrating at Crediton. On the 9th, though there was snow on the ground and it was bitter cold, Cromwell took a brigade to Bovey Tracey where at about six in the evening he surprised part of Lord Wentworth's brigade, taking about 50 men and 400 horses besides seven cornets. This raid led the Royalists to break up the blockade of Plymouth.

Meanwhile, the Commons having gradually assumed all the pre-rogatives of sovereignty, proceeded to reward their supporters. Cromwell for his 'unwearied and faithful services' was to receive an estate of £2,500 per annum for himself and his heirs, the Marquis of Worcester's manors of Abberston and Itchell in Hampshire being voted him, besides £500 to buy 'horse and furniture'. At the same time (23 January) his commission as lieutenant-general was extended for a further six months.

At Exeter Sir John Berkeley still held out, and Lord Hopton man-aged to assemble 3,300 horse and 1,890 foot with provisions for his relief. Leaving Sir Hardress Waller to blockade that city, Fairfax marched on 10 February to meet the Cavaliers.

Hopton reached Torrington, which is built on a steep hill, and barricaded the entrances to the town with ramparts of earth, placing an outpost of dragoons at Stevenstone Park, a mile to his east. On the 16th the Parliamentarians advanced by way of Ring Ash and, falling on Hopton's dragoons, drove them back into Torrington. It was Fairfax's intention to attack after a reconnaissance in daylight, which was wise, for the Royalist position was very strong, and if Hopton had had as many foot as he had horse, would have been a very hard nut to crack.

Soon after dark Fairfax sent Cromwell to inspect his outposts, and the latter deduced from the noise he heard coming from the town that the Cavaliers were about to withdraw. He sent a patrol to test the defences, and when the Cornish fired on it a general fire-fight ensued. For two hours a desperate hand-to-hand fight raged at the barricades, but in the end the Royalist infantry broke. Their cavalry charged through the streets, and at the height of the *mêlée*, Hopton's gunpowder, which was stored in the church, blew up, Fairfax nearly being killed by the explosion. The Cavaliers withdrew west-wards and on 14 March Hopton surrendered at Truro and the war was virtually over. Oxford was to hold out until 24 June, and some isolated strongholds much longer—but the King's last field army under the silver-haired old Astley had surrendered at Stow-on-the-Wold on 21 March.

13 MRS. IRETON—CROMWELL'S ELDEST DAUGHTER, BRIDGET
From the portrait by Sir Peter Lely

9 KING, PARLIAMENT AND ARMY

Gentlemen, ye may now sit down and play, for you have done all your work, if you fall not out among yourselves.

LORD ASTLEY *to his captors at Stow-on-the-Wold, 21 March 1646*

WHEN the war ended, Oliver, at 47, was of an age where a man's mind and character are fully developed. The last six years, replete with action both political and military, had been crowded with experience. His knowledge of the human heart, and his physical powers, were now at their zenith. He had become a loquacious, if unpolished, orator. There is abundant evidence that in his political life he was slow to act before he had thought out a problem and could see his way clear, but his military service had developed his power of quick decision. The religion which he fought for had sustained him in the crises of the war and had brought him through triumphant. His temper was as fiery as ever, but that is no grave drawback to a military commander in time of war.

In the summer of 1646 his family moved from Ely to Drury Lane. His old mother was still alive and so were his wife, two sons and four daughters. Richard and Henry had been to Felsted Grammar School, and had then joined the Army. Richard was serving in Fairfax's Lifeguard and was also at Lincoln's Inn. Henry was to become a captain in Colonel Thomas Harrison's regiment. Bridget (Biddy) and Elizabeth, both serious, religious young ladies, were married in 1646, the one to Ireton, the other, who seems to have been Oliver's favourite child, to John Claypole, a Northamptonshire gentleman. Cromwell's fortune was now sufficient for him to give Elizabeth a generous dowry: £1,250. He loved his Puritan daughters. In a rather charming letter to the newly-wed Bridget he writes: 'Dear Heart, press on, let not husband, let not anything cool thy affections after Christ.' Her sister, Elizabeth, he tells her, 'sees her own vanity and carnal mind, bewailing it . . .'

★   ★   ★

The Parliament to which Cromwell returned from the Army in 1646 was very different from that to which he had first been elected twenty years earlier, and indeed very different to that of 1640. The vacancies created by the ejection of Royalist members were filled up in 1645 and 1646, many of them by friends and fellow-officers, Ireton, Fleetwood, Fairfax. There was now a strong Independent party in the House, but the majority were still Presbyterian members of the propertied classes. In the Army, on the other hand, things were quite otherwise. There the Independents had the upper hand, and to most of them Presbyterianism was almost as bad as Episcopacy.

The war over, Parliament, not unreasonably, wished to reduce the Army. Many regiments were still needed in Ireland, and some for garrisons in England, but the rest must be disbanded. The soldiers, however, were not so simple as to depart without being paid their arrears, which in March 1647 were very considerable, for the horse had received nothing for forty-three weeks, and the foot for eighteen. Parliament, however, was only prepared to produce six weeks' pay. Its resources were strained, for £400,000 had recently been paid to the Scots, who in return, had re-crossed the border in January, handing over the captive King. The policy of Parliament was dishonest and short-sighted, and it brought matters to a head.

Oddly enough, both Fairfax and Cromwell were ill at the time when Parliament was concocting its plan to reduce the New Model, and since neither would have allowed their men to be so shabbily treated without comment, the fact is of importance. In the Commons, Denzil Holles, who hated Cromwell, and Sir Philip Stapleton, who hated the New Model—'that evil army' he had called it— were in the ascendant. 'There want not in all places men who have so much malice against the army as besots them', Oliver told his General in March. 'Upon the Fast-day divers soldiers were raised, both horse and foot, near two hundred in Covent Garden, to prevent us soldiers from cutting the Presbyterians' throats! These are fine tricks to mock God with.'

Even so, there is no evidence that at this stage Oliver contemplated resisting the policy of Parliament. On the contrary, the first solution that suggested itself was to take a contingent to fight for the Elector Palatine, and in March or April he had long conferences with the Calvinist prince. John Lilburne wrote to Cromwell (25 March) complaining that he would not suffer the Army to petition until the

soldiers had laid down their arms; 'because forsooth you have engaged to the House they shall lay down their arms whenever it shall
command them'. When in May, Cromwell, Ireton and Skippon
were sent to the headquarters at Saffron Walden to examine the
grievances of the soldiers, he laboured to persuade them to submit
to Parliament. 'If that authority falls to nothing, nothing can follow
but confusion' (16 May). On their return the commissioners reported that they found the Army 'under a deep sense of some suffering'. On the 21st, receiving the thanks of the Commons, he told
them that although the soldiers would not go to Ireland, he thought
they would disband quietly. The House was now prepared to redress
some of the minor grievances of the soldiery, but money was still
not to be heard of, and on 27 May Parliament insisted on immediate
disbandment. To prevent trouble, this was to take place at widely
different places, beginning on 1 June with Fairfax's own regiment.
The Army, not so easily snared, now concentrated at Newmarket.

But Parliament, in its unwisdom, felt fully capable of quelling the
victors of Naseby by force. The Scots were to be called in; the City
militia was under Presbyterian control, the King, now at Holmby
House in Northamptonshire, was to be brought to London.

In this crisis Cromwell could no longer keep a foot in each camp.
He had to decide whether to throw in his lot with Parliament or
Army, Presbyterian or Independent. By alienating the Army, Par-
liament had led into the hands of the Royalists. If the King could
now play off the one against the other, the fruits of four years' war
would be lost. At the end of May secret meetings took place at
Cromwell's new home in Drury Lane, and on the 31st Cornet
George Joyce of Fairfax's Lifeguard received orders to seize the
Train of Artillery at Oxford and then secure the person of the King.
It looks as if he received these orders from Oliver, but there is no
real evidence on the point, and even though the Member for Cambridge had now thrown in his lot with the Army it was not with any
intention of overthrowing the Parliament. Rather he hoped to play
the role of mediator.

Joyce reached Holmby at midnight on 2 June. It was not until the
3rd that Cromwell set out for Newmarket; it is curious to reflect
that had he remained in the capital his Parliamentary colleagues
would very likely have lodged him in the Tower. When he arrived

the Army was concentrated on Kentford Heath, where the men bound themselves by a solemn engagement not to disband until their rights were secured. A General Council composed of the generals and two officers and two privates from each regiment was to represent the Army in political matters and to negotiate with Parliament. In purely military matters the Army still recognized the authority of Fairfax and the Council of War, in which Lieutenant-General Cromwell was the *primum mobile*. Discipline, which had suffered as a consequence of the uncertainty prevailing in recent weeks, was apparently restored, and in Firth's view the General Council became no more than a debating society. In July Lilburne was to reproach Cromwell for this. 'You have robbed, by your unjust subtlety and shifting tricks, the honest and gallant Agitators of all their power and authority, and solely placed it in a thing called a council of war.' For all that it seems that Cromwell was compelled to take a lead at this time, for had he not, the soldiers and the Agitators were determined to 'go their way without him'.

With the King in the hands of the Army, which now moved forward to Triploe Heath near Cambridge, the Parliament's position had greatly deteriorated. Too late the Houses began to offer concessions, including the full payment of arrears, but what would have been welcomed in May was rejected in June. The Army pushed on to St. Albans. Beyond doubt the plan of the Presbyterian leaders to recall the Scots was known. In May the soldiers would have settled for their arrears. Now nothing short of a constitutional settlement would suffice. A letter to the City of London, signed by all the principal officers, and perhaps drafted by Oliver himself, sets forth their point of view.

> As Englishmen—and surely our being soldiers hath not stripped us of that interest, though our malicious enemies would have it so—we desire a settlement of the peace of the Kingdom and of the liberties of the subject, according to the votes and declarations of Parliament, which before we took arms, were by the Parliament used as arguments to invite us and divers of our dear friends out; some of whom have lost their lives in this war.

As passions rose, the demands of the Army became more precise. Ireton now formulated a Declaration, signed on 14 June, in which the Army sought the purging of Parliament, and the choice of an entirely new House. Eleven members were to be proscribed as enemies of the state. Denzil Holles, who was one of them, wrote: 'here they first took upon them openly to intermeddle with the business of the kingdom'. Cromwell, who only the day before, had signed the letter saying 'we desire as much as any to maintain the authority of Parliament', was among those who signed the Declaration. No doubt his talented son-in-law, who evidently saw that the absolutism of Parliament was as much an evil as that of the King, had brought him to change his position.

Parliament sought to temporize; the eleven impeached members voluntarily withdrew, and negotiations began at High Wycombe on 1 July. This delay was not at all to the taste of the Agitators who were all for marching on London. This Cromwell resisted: 'Whatsoever we get by a treaty will be firm and durable. . . . That you have by force I look upon it as nothing' (16 July). He had his way and the Council of the Army agreed to postpone their march. Instead they forwarded to London the scheme known as the 'Heads of the Proposals', which had been drafted by Ireton and Major-General Lambert. This document was intended as a basis for discussion and negotiation between King, Parliament and Army.

The Parliament now abandoned all attempt at resistance, but London did not. On 26 July a mob besieged the Houses threatening the members with violence and hotly opposing any measures to conciliate the Army. Both Speakers, eight Peers—practically all that remained of the Lords—and fifty-seven members of the Commons now took refuge with the Army, declaring that Parliament was no longer free.

The Presbyterians still showed fight, Holles and the other impeached members resumed their places in Parliament, and the City forces were mobilized under Major-General Massey. But these men were no match for the New Model, and when Fairfax reached Hounslow all resistance collapsed. On 6 August Cromwell rode into London at the head of his cavalry, and the Presbyterian leaders fled to the Continent.

★   ★   ★

Parliament had failed lamentably to achieve a settlement, but there was still the King, and on him the hopes of the Army were now centred. The policy of the general was to come to terms with Charles, but it was based on the misconception that he would take their overtures seriously. To the King, Fairfax was still the 'brutish general' of the New Model, while Cromwell, whom Archbishop Williams had warned him against so long since, had always had 'a bad press' with the Royalists. The man who had sacked Basing, the desecrator of cathedrals, was not exactly *persona grata* with the monarch.

The chief result of the negotiations which followed was to sow mistrust of the generals in the hearts of their only true supporters, the soldiers.

Yet the settlement already outlined in the Heads of the Proposals was a magnanimous one, with something in it to appeal to all parties. The estates of Cavaliers were to be protected from ruinous sequestration; the Episcopate was to be retained, though shorn of its coercive power; those who wished to use the Prayer-book in church could do so. There was to be toleration for all. The King was to be restored, though the royal power was to be controlled by Parliament.

In September Charles rejected the terms offered to him, and many were against any further negotiations, but though Cromwell and Ireton succeeded in carrying a vote that fresh terms should be offered, the King fled to the Isle of Wight (11 November) before the new proposals could be offered to him. Sir John Berkeley, the Royalist leader who was close to Charles at this time, shows that it was the Scottish envoys who instigated this flight, though Charles may have become convinced that the soldiery were out of hand and that he was in danger of being murdered. Many, however, have attributed the flight to Cromwell's machinations, and Marvell's lines give the traditional view:

> *Twining subtle fears with hope,*
> *He wove a net of such a scope,*
> *That Charles himself might chase*
> *To Carisbrook's narrow case,*
> *That thence the royal actor borne*
> *The tragic scaffold might adorn.*

The idea of bringing the King to the block had not as yet entered Cromwell's mind, even though during the war, when rebels pretended to be fighting 'for King and Parliament'—more forthright than his fellows—he was reported to have said 'if the King were before me I would shoot him as another'.

Cromwell now saw that in hoping to arrive at a permanent settlement by a treaty with the King he had been living in a world of his own. The Royalists had skilfully spread the rumour that Cromwell's price for the King's restoration was an earldom and the Garter, a story generally believed.

In this time of doubt and rumour the discipline of the Army had suffered. Between 15 and 18 November three great reviews were held; Fairfax and Cromwell won over the waverers and entered into a solemn engagement for the redress of military grievances and the reform of Parliament. At Ware (15 December) the generals had mutiny to contend with. Fairfax soon subdued Harrison's regiment, but Colonel Robert Lilburne's was in ugly mood. They were drawn up as for battle with copies of *The Agreement of the People*—a radical scheme of the Levellers'—stuck in their hats, with the motto 'England's Freedom, Soldiers' Rights' printed on the back. Cromwell rode down the ranks, ordering the men to take the papers out of their hats; they refused. This was too much for his hot temper and drawing his sword he dashed alone into the midst of the mutineers. His resolution did the trick; tearing the papers from their hats, the men craved for mercy. A dozen were tried on the spot, and a corporal was shot at the head of the regiment, an example which sufficed to reduce the rest to obedience, and restore normal military discipline. The Army Council was disbanded.

On 3 January 1648 the King rejected four bills which Parliament had presented to him as their ultimatum. In the debate that followed Cromwell played a leading part: 'The army now expected that parliament should govern and defend the Kingdom by their own power and resolution, and not teach the people any longer to expect safety and government from an obstinate man whose heart God had hardened'. By trying to play off Army against Parliament, Charles had now succeeded in uniting both against him, for if either trusted him before, neither did so now. The upshot was that Parliament voted that no further addresses should be made to the King, and excluded the representatives of Scotland from the Committee of Both Kingdoms. This made war with Scotland inevitable, and in the following months Cromwell busied himself with the necessary preparations.

His work was to some extent hindered by the distrust with which many of his old associates now regarded him. On 19 January 1648, John Lilburne, speaking at the bar of the House, accused him of apostasy, and denounced his underhand dealings with the King. These suspicions, as Ludlow tells us, troubled Cromwell greatly. He was living in King Street at this time, and here a conference was held to discuss the question of the future government of the Kingdom. He and 'the grandees . . . kept themselves in the clouds, and would not declare their judgments . . .'—this was ever Oliver's way in political matters. 'The Commonwealths-men declared that monarchy was neither good in itself nor for us . . .', Ludlow continues, 'arguing from the 8th chapter and 8th verse of the first Book of Samuel, where the rejecting of the Judges, and the choice of a King, was charged upon the Israelites by God himself as a rejection of him; . . .'

A grave and lengthy argument was eventually concluded by the host, with a piece of horseplay reminiscent of his younger days, when 'having learned what he could of the principles and inclinations of those present', he took up a cushion and flung it at Ludlow's head, and then ran down the stairs; but Ludlow, not to be outdone, 'overtook him with another, which made him hasten down faster than he desired'. The way ahead was dark indeed, and in endless conferences, prayer-meetings and sermonizings these Puritan warriors sought the light.

I do not ask to see the distant scene,
One step enough for me.

A great prayer-meeting was held at their headquarters at Windsor at the end of April 1648, when the Army leaders came to the conclusion that all their troubles were due to 'those cursed carnal conferences with the king', and determined that 'it was their duty, if ever the Lord brought them back in peace, to call Charles Stuart, that man of blood, to account for all the blood he had shed and the mischief he had done to his utmost, against the Lord's cause and people in these poor nations'.

Charles for his part had laid his plans three months earlier. On 26

December he and the Scottish Commissioners had secretly signed the agreement known as 'the Engagement', an alliance of Royalist and Scot which was to bring about the Second Civil War.

16 Cromwell's House: Clerkenwell Close

10 THE SECOND CIVIL WAR AND THE EXECUTION OF KING CHARLES

I tell you we will cut off his head, with the crown on it.

THE first outbreak was in South Wales, and was a somewhat premature revolt of men who had fought for Parliament in the First Civil War. In March Colonel John Poyer declared for the King and was soon joined by Rowland Laugharne. By April it was known that the Scots were raising an army to invade England, and at the end of that month the Royalists seized Carlisle and Berwick. Fairfax decided to deal with the Scots in person, and sent Cromwell to put down the rising in Wales. Before Oliver could take the field, Colonel Horton had broken the back of the rebellion by his victory at St.

Fagans (8 May). It only remained to mop up. Colonel Ewer stormed Chepstow on 25 May, and Horton took Tenby at the end of the month. Only at Pembroke did the Royalists manage to delay the inevitable. Several assaults were beaten off with loss. Cromwell had only a few small guns, and was unable to make an adequate breach in the massive mediaeval walls. But starvation did his work, and on 11 July the garrison surrendered to the 'mercy of the Parliament'. Colonel Poyer and some of his ex-Roundhead officers were, however, exempted from mercy by Oliver, having 'sinned against so much light and against so many evidences of Divine Presence going along with and prospering a righteous cause, in the management of which they themselves had a share'.

Elsewhere the rising was proving formidable. At the end of May there was a serious outbreak in Kent, and the fleet in the Downs declared for the King. Fairfax stormed Maidstone on 1 June, but the remnant of the Royalists crossed the Thames and flung themselves into Colchester, where they improvised a defence and held out until 28 August.

In several other counties the Royalists came out in arms, and on 8 July Hamilton crossed the border with some 10,000 men, to be joined by Langdale and Musgrave with considerable numbers of English Royalists. While he was recruiting, the Duke contented himself with besieging castles in the north, but by mid-August he was ready to thrust southwards through Lancashire. By this time Cromwell was hastening north to meet him.

Marching via Carmarthen, Gloucester, Warwick, Leicester and Nottingham, he joined Lambert near Knaresborough on 12 August. The Royalists had seized Pontefract and Scarborough castles, and after detaching regiments to mask these fortresses, Cromwell and Lambert could only muster about 9,000 men, including some 3,000 horse. The ragged soldiers had seen no pay for months, though Oliver had at least managed to provide new shoes and stockings at Leicester. The Roundhead infantry had behaved well, covering the 260 miles from Pembroke to Pontefract in 27 days, and, despite their wants, refraining from plunder. There was nothing the matter with their discipline, when there was action in the offing. Indeed it was in the words of Captain John Hodgson, who served in it, a 'fine smart army, fit for action'.

Hamilton had the advantage of numbers, but nothing else. His men were great plunderers. 'The Scotch', wrote Hesilrige, now Governor of Newcastle, 'take all–movables, cows, sheep and all household stuff to the very pothooks; they take children and make their parents pay ransom for them, and force women before their friends' faces'. Burnet tells us that 'not the fifth man could handle pike or musket'. The horses were good, but the troopers raw and un-disciplined. They had 'not so much as one field-piece, very little ammunition, and very few horse to carry it . . .' The Royalist risings had found Hamilton unprepared.

At first, Cromwell, very reasonably, expected that Hamilton would endeavour to relieve Pontefract, but learning that the Scots were advancing through Lancashire, he crossed the Pennines via Skipton (A. 59), reaching Gisburn on 15 August. Next day he pushed on down the valley of the Ribble. He had the alternative of trying to bar Hamilton's progress somewhere south of the river, or of thrust-ing at Preston. Determined to bring on a decisive battle, he chose the latter course. 'It was thought that to engage the enemy to fight was our business.' He was bent, moreover, on the annihilation of the Duke's army: 'Upon deliberate advice we chose rather to put our-selves between their army and Scotland'.

On the night of 16 August the Roundheads encamped at Stony-hurst, about nine miles from Preston, where his opponent lay with some 10,000 foot and 1,500 horse. The Lieutenant-General, the Earl of Callander, with most of the Scottish horse, had pushed on ahead, and was nearing Wigan, seventeen miles further south. Incredible though it may seem, the rearguard, Major-General Munro with 3,000 Scottish veterans from Ulster, and Musgrave's English Cava-liers, were still near Kirkby Lonsdale, fully thirty miles north of the main body. But between Hamilton and Cromwell lay that dour Yorkshire Roman Catholic, Sir Marmaduke Langdale, with 600 horse and 3,000 foot. Langdale warned the Duke of Cromwell's approach, but Hamilton was pleased to believe himself threatened by nothing more formidable than the militia of Lancashire. Thus early on the morning of Thursday, 17 August 1648, Oliver came driving in on the flank guard of an army whose commander had allowed it to get strung out over some fifty miles of country.

Outnumbered by nearly three to one, Langdale was soon sending urgent appeals to Hamilton, but no help came. Callander rode on to Wigan, while Hamilton's foot remained inactive. The English Cavaliers were left to fight it out on their own. Well posted in hedges and fields, Langdale held on for four hours, 'often coming to push of pike and close firing', and making 'though he was worsted, very stiff and sturdy resistance'. After a long struggle, the Roundhead reserve, Colonel Ralph Assheton and his Lancashire levies, went in, and the Cavaliers fell back into Preston, where Hamilton and his Lifeguard joined in the fray. Cromwell's own regiment, seconded by Colonel Thomas Harrison's charged through the town. Hamilton, in his turn, counter-charged three times, but the Ironsides beat him back. The Duke was compelled to save himself by swimming the Ribble. Cromwell, holding the bridges over both Ribble and Darwen, was astride the road to Scotland. He had already taken 4,000 prisoners.

Hamilton still outnumbered Oliver; many of his infantry had not yet fired a shot, and the vanguard of cavalry at Wigan had not yet been engaged. After a conference in the saddle, the Scots commanders decided to depart to Wigan. 'Our march', wrote one of them, 'was very sad, the way being exceeding deep, the soldiers both wet, hungry, and weary, and all looked on their business as half ruined.' Well they might, for every mile was taking them further from home.

Next morning, Cromwell, leaving the Lancashire militia to guard his captives at Preston, set out in pursuit. The Scottish horse, though they had managed to miss their infantry during the night, now covered their withdrawal with fair success; the gallant Colonel, Francis Thornhagh, who led Cromwell's advance, being mortally wounded by one of their lancers.

Reaching Wigan, Hamilton and his officers decided that the moor did not offer a suitable defensive position, and pushed on to Warrington, ten miles further south—another night march. Conditions were not good for either side. 'We lay that night in the field', wrote Cromwell, 'close by the enemy, being very dirty and weary, and having marched twelve miles of such ground as I never rode in my life, the day being very wet.' Next day he caught up with the Scottish infantry at Winwick, some three miles from Warrington:

> We held them in dispute, [he writes], till our army came up, they maintaining the pass with great resolution for many hours, ours and theirs

coming to push of pike and very close charges, which forced us to give ground; but our men by the blessing of God quickly recovered it, and charging very home upon them, beat them from their standing. We killed about a thousand of them, and took, as we believe, about two thousand prisoners.

The end was near. General Baillie and the Scottish infantry now surrendered. Hamilton, with perhaps 3,000 horse, made a bid to join Lord Byron, who was up in arms in Nottinghamshire, but Oliver sent off Lambert and four regiments of horse in pursuit, and the poor remains of this army capitulated at Uttoxeter on the 25th. Three days later, Colchester surrendered to Fairfax, and the Second Civil War was nearly over.

Munro meanwhile had beaten a retreat, and it only remained to recover Berwick and Carlisle. The Marquis of Argyll, with whom Cromwell had an interview on 22 September, was now in power and was glad enough to come to terms. Oliver was invited to Edinburgh, where the presence of his cavalry helped to consolidate the position of the new government. The Covenanters ousted the Engagers, and Cromwell was able to report that Scotland was like to become a better neighbour.

The Second Civil War left bitter feelings in Cromwell's heart, not only against renegade Roundheads like Poyer who had 'sinned against so much light', but against the Cavaliers, who had not accepted their defeat in the First War, and had brought in the Scots.

> This, [quoth he] is a more prodigious treason than any that hath been perfected before; because the former quarrel was that Englishmen might rule over one another, this to vassalise us to a foreign nation. And their fault that appeared in this summer's business is certainly double to theirs who were in the first, because it is the repetition of the same offence against all the witnesses that God hath borne.

Above all, it was with the King himself that they must settle.

Cromwell was in no hurry to return south. At a time when political problems of great complexity were looming on the horizon, he was glad of a pretext to stay away from London. Pontefract Castle still held out, and Oliver now busied himself with the siege—and no doubt with much meditation also. Denzil Holles was now back in Westminster, at the head of a party which had learned so little from events that they had reopened negotiations with the King. With the wounds of the Second Civil War still fresh, this was to Cromwell, as he wrote on 6 November, 'an accursed thing': few of the New Model can have thought otherwise. The Levellers were already demanding the deposition of King Charles, and on 18 November Fairfax, on behalf of the Army, forwarded a Remonstrance to Parliament demanding his trial as 'the grand author of our troubles'. The northern army was at one with Fairfax's men in holding that impartial justice must be meted out to all offenders. 'I do in all, from my heart, concur with them', wrote Cromwell. Sustained success had fortified his dogmatic Calvinistic convictions. 'Let us look into providences: surely they mean somewhat, ... They hang so together; have been so constant, so clear and unclouded.' In other words: 'We have won so often; we must be in the right.' Fairfax now ordered his Lieutenant-General south, and handing over the command at Pontefract to Lambert—who would have been quite capable of conducting the siege from the first—Oliver returned to take his place at Westminster.

It was a very different assembly that Cromwell found on his arrival, for while he had been wrestling with his conscience, some of his brother-officers, including his son-in-law, Ireton, had seen the writing on the wall somewhat sooner, and one of them, Colonel Pride the drayman, had taken it upon himself, on 6 December, the day before Oliver arrived in the capital, to administer 'Pride's Purge'. Supported by a file of musketeers, the Colonel had arrested forty-five members and excluded ninety-six others. The Presbyterian leaders were gone. All who might oppose the trial of a King were gone too.

This drastic solution was not one that Cromwell himself had contemplated, but he was quick to give his support: 'he had not been acquainted with this design, but since it was done he was glad of it, and would endeavour to maintain it'.

The execution of the King, which took place on 30 January 1649, only eight weeks after Cromwell's return from the north, was chiefly the work of two men, Ireton and Cromwell himself. Accepting the *fait accompli* of Pride's Purge, fortified by long meditation, and by the convincing arguments of his clever son-in-law, at some stage though exactly when none can tell, Oliver decided that the King must die. Before he had made up his mind, he was open to every sort of argument: a decision once reached, his mind was as concrete. So it was now. He threw himself with all his passionate, Messianic vigour into the business of turning a monarch into a martyr. And an ugly tale it is, for even though the accounts that survive are far from satisfactory, much emerges that reflects grave discredit on Cromwell and the New Model Army, though the General, Fairfax, played little part in all this, for his wife was a Royalist. Fairfax indeed had the sense to point out that the execution of one King would merely give the nation another in the person of his son—then safe in Holland.

A Dutch lawyer, one Dorislaus, was found to frame the indictment, and what remained of the Commons meekly produced an ordinance creating a tribunal of 135 Commissioners—over half of whom had the wit to avoid serving—to try the King.

On 20 January the trial began. The Commissioners were sitting in the Painted Chamber when the news came that Charles was landing at the steps:

> At which Cromwell ran to the window, looking on the King as he came up the garden; he turned as white as the wall . . . then turning to the board said thus: 'My masters, he is come, he is come, and now we are doing that great work that the whole nation will be full of. Therefore I desire you to let us resolve here what answer we shall give the King when he comes before us, for the first question he will ask us will be by what authority and commision we do try him?' For a time no one answered. Then after a little space, Henry Marten rose up and said 'In the name of the Commons in Parliament assembled and all the good people of England'.

Had he replied 'In the name of the Rump and the New Model Army' it would have been nearer the mark.

The trial took place in Westminster Hall. The judges in their ordinary attire, sat on four or five tiers of benches covered with scarlet cloth. Cromwell sat in the back row on one side of the escutcheon bearing the arms of the Commonwealth of England. Overlooking the court were small galleries for important spectators, but the mass of onlookers, well guarded by soldiers in the gangways, was at the end of the hall.

The King, who wore his hat throughout, paid no respect to the court, and while the charge was read, sat in his chair, looking about him. Once he got up to look at the guards and spectators 'and after sat down, looking very sternly, and with a countenance not at all moved, till these words '*Charles Stuart to be a tyrant*', traitor, etc., were read; at which he laughed, as he sat, in the face of the court'.

Throughout the proceedings Charles refused to admit the jurisdiction of the court, or to plead.

> It is not my case alone, [he said]; it is the freedom of the people of England; and do you pretend what you will, I stand more for their liberties. For if power without law may make laws, may alter the fundamental laws of the Kingdom, I do not know what subject he is in England that can be sure of his life, or anything that he calls his own.

Not only the legality but the conduct of the trial evidently left something to be desired. When the president, Serjeant John Bradshaw, called upon the King to answer the charge as framed by Marten, Lady Fairfax, one of the spectators, intervened with: 'It's a lie, not half, nor a quarter of the people of England! Oliver Cromwell is a rogue and a traitor!' Enraged by this interruption, Colonel Axtell lost his head and ordered his men to fire into the gallery— an order they had the sense to disobey. Lady Fairfax was persuaded to depart, but she had had her say.

On 27 January, Bradshaw, clad for the occasion in a scarlet gown, delivered sentence. The King still refused to plead, but declared that he had something to say. After a brief consultation the court refused to hear him, and Bradshaw read the sentence, Cromwell and the other commissioners rising to give their assent. Once more Charles demanded a hearing.

'Sir', quoth Bradshaw, 'you are not to be heard after sentence', and when the King insisted, harshly added, 'Guard, withdraw your prisoner.'

'I am not suffered to speak', said the King. 'Expect what justice other people will have.' He was led from the court between ranks of soldiers, Axtell had ordered them to set up a cry of 'Justice! Justice! Execution! Execution!' some of them reviling him, and others blowing their tobacco smoke in his face. The temper of the populace was different: some wept for him, and many prayed.

A liuely Reprefentation of the manner how his late Majefty was beheaded uppon the Scaffold Ian 30 1648.

17 THE EXECUTION OF CHARLES I
From a contemporary print

18 THE BATTLE OF DUNBAR, 1650
Detail from a contemporary engraving by Payne Fisher

In all this Cromwell and Ireton were, it seems, the moving figures. Algernon Sidney has related how being nominated as one of the judges and arguing that 'the King could be tried by no court' and 'that no man could be tried by that court'; Cromwell replied, 'I tell you we will cut off his head, with the crown on it . . .'

On 30 January 1649 the axe fell.

11   IRELAND, 1649–1650

The black curse of Cromwell

ON 15 March 1649 the Council of State selected Cromwell to command in Ireland. He was to be Lord-Lieutenant and Commander-in-Chief for three years with a total salary of £13,000 per annum, and an army 12,000 strong.

Cromwell landed at Dublin on 15 August to find himself already 'master of the field'. Colonel Michael Jones, the governor of Dublin, had surprised the Royalist camp at Rathmines on 2 August and inflicted 5,000 casualties on them. Cromwell wrote of it as an 'astonishing mercy', and it meant that Ormonde, the Royalist leader could no longer face him in battle.

Cromwell now overhauled his army. On 23 August he published a proclamation against profane swearing, cursing and drunkenness, and next day another prohibiting pillage and promising the country folk a free market in his camp. This done he marched on Drogheda. The garrison, 2,800 strong, were the pick of Ormonde's army, under a one-legged catholic, Sir Arthur Aston, a testy and imperious veteran of the Thirty Years War, of Edgehill and Newbury, who had once been the much detested Royalist governor of Oxford.

Cromwell arrived before this stronghold on 3 September, and by the 10th had made two small breaches in the south wall. About five o'clock of the following afternoon, after a cannonade, Cromwell ordered his men to storm. Twice they were beaten back, but Oliver himself led them to a third assault, which at last broke in. At first

some prisoners were taken, but Cromwell was in savage mood. Let
him tell his own story:

> The enemy retreated, divers of them, into the Mill Mount; a place
> very strong and of difficult access, being exceedingly high, having a
> good graft [ditch], and strongly palisaded. The Governor, Sir Arthur
> Aston, and divers considerable officers being there, our men, getting
> up to them, were ordered by me to put them all to the sword. And in-
> deed, being in the heat of action, I forbade them to spare any that were
> in arms in the town, and I think that night they put to the sword about
> 2,000 men . . .

Some held out in the west gate and in churches. 'These, being summoned to yield to mercy, refused, whereupon I ordered the steeple
of St. Peter's church to be fired, where one of them was heard to say
in the midst of the flames: "God damn me, God confound me: I
burn, I burn".'

The Roundhead soldiers ranged through the streets in a mood no
less savage than that of their commander, killing not only the garrison but many civilians with every circumstance of horror. One
example must suffice to show the hideous nature of this storm.
Thomas Wood, formerly a Royalist lieutenant, but now an officer
in Ingoldsby's regiment, was at the storming of a church. When they
had killed everyone there,

> . . . they went into the vaults underneath where all the flower and
> choicest of the women and ladies had hid themselves. One of these, a
> most handsome virgin and arrayed in costly and gorgeous apparel,
> kneeled down to Tho. Wood with tears and prayers to save her life:
> and being strucken with a profound pity, [he] took her under his arm,
> went with her out of the church, with intentions to put her over the
> works and to let her shift for her self; but then a soldier perceiving his
> intentions, he ran his sword up her belly or fundament.

There is an element of self-justification in Cromwell's letter about
these atrocities; they were done 'in the heat of action'; the slaughter
'. . . will tend to prevent the effusion of blood for the future, which
are the satisfactory grounds to such actions, which otherwise cannot
but work remorse and regret'. It is true that Trim and Dundalk were
immediately abandoned, but later, at Waterford and Clonmel, the
garrisons, rendered desperate by this cruelty, held out beyond all
expectation. The defender of a fortress who resists after a practicable
breach has been made can only expect to see his garrison slaughtered.

The Duke of Wellington himself has given his opinion that: 'The practice of refusing quarter to a garrison which stands an assault is not a useless effusion of blood.' All warfare is designed to change the enemy's mind, to make him think he is beaten, to make him give up the struggle. Atrocities can only be justified if they contribute to this end. The horrors of Drogheda struck terror into Ormonde's men for a time, but before many months were past panic was replaced by grim resolution.

Cromwell now struck at Wexford, which he reached on 1 October. The town resisted after the castle had fallen, and in the storm 2,000 soldiers and civilians were massacred. Cromwell neither ordered nor condemned this slaughter:

> I was intending better to this place than so great a ruin, hoping the town might be of more use to you and your army, yet God would not have it so; but, by an unexpected providence in His righteous justice, brought a just judgment upon them; causing them to become a prey to the soldier, who in their piracies had made preys of so many families, and made with their bloods to answer the cruelties which they had exercised upon the lives of divers poor Protestants.

Ross surrendered after a two-day siege (19 October), but Waterford held out stoutly and on 2 December Cromwell was compelled to raise the siege. Sickness and foul weather had wrought havoc. Michael Jones had died of the plague, and Colonel Horton, the victor of St. Fagans (1648), had succumbed to the local form of malaria. 'I scarce have one officer of forty amongst us that hath not been sick', wrote Cromwell, 'and how many considerable ones we have lost is no little thought of heart to us.' He himself fell ill. The Lord was turning his face from his anointed.

Nevertheless, the Parliamentarians had won other successes. Colonel Venables had relieved Londonderry in September, and Lord Broghill had taken Cork. But the interior was as yet unconquered. 'Though God hath blessed you with a great longitude of land along the shore, yet hath it but little depth into the country.'

Cromwell took the field early in 1650. Cashel and Cahir fell in February and Kilkenny on 27 March. But at Clonmel the Ironsides met their match in 'an old surly Spanish soldier', Hugh O'Neill, who repulsed them with the loss of some 2,000 men. Ireton considered this defeat 'the heaviest we ever endured either in England or here'.

Having spent almost all their ammunition the garrison slipped out by night and got clear away to Waterford. The mayor handed over the town to an irate Oliver on 10 May.

Cromwell had been recalled by Parliament as early as 8 January, for war with Scotland was expected, but not until Clonmel had fallen did he obey the summons, handing over the command to Ireton. The war lingered on for another two years, but the back of the resistance was broken.

Cromwell's success in Ireland, such as it was, was purely military. His political settlement was neither liberal nor successful. Although he did not originate the policy of the wholesale transplantation of the Irish to the barren wastes of Connaught, he was strongly in favour of colonizing Ireland with new settlers from England. When his men had slaughtered the unfortunate inhabitants of Wexford he was quick to point out its possibilities as a colony. He wrote to New England inviting 'godly people and ministers' to come to Ireland, and found a number to do so. The Parliament's policy of land forfeiture also found favour in his eyes. Those who had been in arms were to suffer for it in their estates as the Cavaliers did in England. By the wholesale confiscation of land he was able to pay the adventurers who had lent money for the campaign, and his soldiers who had taken part in it.

To Cromwell the Irish were no better than beasts. In 1655, when his son Henry was Lord Deputy, he tried to arrange for a thousand 'young Irish wenches' to be sent to Jamaica for the use of the new settlers. Despite the oft-quoted assertion: 'I meddle not with any man's conscience . . .', the catholics were harried unmercifully, their priests hunted down, the mass proscribed. The incredible truth is that Cromwell actually hoped for their conversion. 'We find the people very greedy after the word, and flocking to christian meetings, much of that prejudice which lies upon the people in England being a stranger to their minds. I mind you the rather of this because it is a sweet symptom, if not an earnest of the good we expect.' But in fact his policy of conversion was an utter failure. In Buchan's words, 'the Catholic church drew fresh strength from its sufferings'.

Yet some good can be found in his settlement. Ireland was given equal trading rights with England, similar taxation, and Parliamentary union. The administration of justice was improved, and Trinity

College endowed, though all this counted for little in the eyes of the oppressed Irish.

It is easy to excuse Cromwell's cruelty and short-sightedness by saying that his policy was merely an extension of Tudor policy and of that laid down in 1642 by the Long Parliament. Of what use are great men if they cannot rise above the narrow prejudices of their generation? The truth is that at least two of his contemporaries, Ormonde and Strafford, understood Ireland better than did Oliver. Though it would have been far better for Ireland's future and for Cromwell's fame had he never set foot on her shores, one thing at least he had achieved: Ireland was no longer a potential base for a Royalist reconquest of England.

Marvell's lines:

> And now the Irish are ashamed
> To see themselves in one year tamed:
> So much one man can do
> That does both act and know.

may represent contemporary English opinion of Cromwell's achievement in Ireland, but in truth he had done much harm and little good. Of the massacres at Drogheda and Wexford, Sir Charles Firth, no unfavourable critic, wrote: 'their memory still helps to separate the two races Cromwell wished to unite'.

19 Cromwell's House in Whitehall

Now let God arise, and his enemies shall be scattered.

WHEN Cromwell and Ireton induced the commissioners to sign King Charles's death-warrant they were sending not only their own King, but the King of Scots to the block.

Six days after the execution at Whitehall, the Scottish estates proclaimed Charles II King. '*Le roi est mort, vive le roi!*' They in their turn exceeded their powers, for they proclaimed him King, not of Scotland alone, but of Great Britain, France and Ireland. Their envoys in England demanded his recognition there and were immediately expelled by the Long Parliament, which declared that they had laid 'the grounds of a new and bloody war'.

In the spring of 1649 Scottish Commissioners visited King Charles II in the Netherlands and demanded not only that he should accept the Covenant and Presbyterianism, but that he should impose them throughout his dominions. Charles at first refused, hoping that Montrose and the Scottish Cavaliers would do his business for him. But the Kirk party was too strong for Montrose, and even before his capture, the King had sailed for Scotland and taken the Covenant. He arrived at Edinburgh in June, 1650.

★   ★   ★

Upon his return from Ireland Cromwell was well received. At Bristol he was welcomed with a triple salute from all the great guns. At Windsor, where he was met by a deputation from Parliament on 31 May, 'he was entertained with many vollies of shot . . .' For his part he showed himself 'very affable and courteous unto all', and admitted anyone that had business to speak with him. Emboldened by his return, the government now suppressed certain Royalist newssheets which had appeared during the past year. The printer of *Mercurius Pragmaticus*, who had invented for Oliver the titles 'Copper Nose', 'The Town Bull of Ely' and 'Nose Almighty', found himself in Newgate.

In mid-June the question of the command in the north came to the fore. Fairfax had no desire to invade 'a neighbour nation, especially our brethren of Scotland, to whom we are engaged in a solemn league and covenant'. Cromwell was, therefore, commissioned as 'captain-general and commander-in-chief of all forces raised and to be raised within the Commonwealth of England', and on 4 July the Council of State declared war on Scotland.

As he went north Cromwell was everywhere treated with great respect. At Leicester the mayor and aldermen entertained him with 'wyne, biskets, suger, beare and tobacko', at York 'a great volley from Clifford's Tower' saluted him. The cheers of the mob left Oliver unimpressed:

'Do not trust to that', he said to Lambert, 'for these very persons would shout as much if you and I were going to be hanged.'

By 10 July he was at Newcastle, where he halted to organize his army of some 16,000 men. During his stay there Cromwell and his officers drew up 'A Declaration of the Army of England upon their March into Scotland To all that are Saints, and Partakers of the Faith of God's Elect, in Scotland', a document in which they justified the execution of the King and protested, somewhat illogically, that they undertook 'this business in fear of God, with bowels full of love, yea, full of pity . . .'

However that may be, the two fundamental points at issue when on 22 July 1650 the English crossed the Tweed, were to settle the questions whether Charles II was to reign, even in Scotland, and whether Presbyterianism was to be the form of religion for both countries.

Cromwell's opponent was to be David Leslie, who had so effectively supported him at Marston Moor, and who had since defeated Montrose at Philiphaugh. He had laid waste the border country, compelling Cromwell to operate near the coast so as to keep in touch with his supply ships. On the afternoon of 25 July the camp was broken up without sound of trumpet or beat of drum, and the army advanced to Cockburnspath, a rough, narrow pass between the sea and the Lammermuirs. Leslie had 27,000 foot and 5,000 horse, but his army had neither the discipline nor the experience of Cromwell's. Many of the best officers, old soldiers and English Cavaliers, were cashiered at the instance of the covenanting zealots, and replaced by 'ministers' sons, clerks, and such other sanctified creatures,

who hardly ever saw or heard of any sword but that of the spirit'
(Walker).

The English reached Dunbar on 26 July and began to land provisions. Next day they marched to Haddington, twelve miles from
Edinburgh, where at last they came in contact with the enemy. On
the 29th Cromwell reconnoitred Leslie's almost impregnable en-
trenched lines covering Leith and Edinburgh. Both sides hoped the
other would attack, but a month of bickering brought no decisive
action. Leslie was taking no risks. By the end of August provisions
became very scarce in the English camp, and there was a great deal
of sickness. Cromwell led his 'poor, shattered, hungry, discouraged
army', back to Dunbar, meaning to fortify the town so that it would
serve as a magazine and a base for future operations. He hoped for
reinforcements from Berwick.

Leslie, following close at his heels, occupied Doon Hill looking down on Dunbar, and seized the passes between that place and
Berwick. The English were now in a worse position than the Parliamentarian army had been at Lostwithiel in 1644. But though the
campaign thus far had been a complete failure, and his strategy had
outrun his administrative means, Cromwell was not Essex. In this
predicament he wrote to Hesilrige on 2 September:

> We are upon an engagement very difficult. The enemy hath blocked
> up our way at the pass at Copperspath [sic], through which we cannot
> get without almost a miracle. He lieth so upon the hills that we know
> not how to come that way without great difficulty; and our lying here
> daily consumeth our men, who fall sick beyond imagination.
> I perceive your forces are not in a capacity for present relief; where-
> fore...it will be well for you to get what forces you can together; and
> the South to help what they can. . . . Our spirits are comfortable
> (praised be the Lord), though our present condition be as it is. . . . Let
> H. Vane know what I write. I would not make it public, lest danger
> should accrue thereby. You know what use to make hereof.

The weather was foul, and the Scots Commissioners soon wearied
of lying in the fields, thinking Leslie 'made not haste enough to
destroy those Sectaries. . . . He told them by lying there all was sure;
but that by engaging in action with gallant and desperate men, all
might be lost, yet they still called on him to fall on'.

Early on 2 September the Scots advanced. There was some skir-
mishing, and some prisoners were interrogated as to whether the

English meant to fight. One boldy asked Leslie what he thought they had come there for.

'How will you fight', said Leslie, 'when you have shipped half your men and all your great guns?'

'Sir', the man answered, 'if you will please to draw down your army to the foot of the hill, you shall find both men and great guns too.'

Cromwell, who estimates Leslie's army at about 6,000 horse and at least 16,000 foot, and his own strength as 3,500 horse and 7,500 foot, continues the story. On Monday evening

> the enemy drew down to their right wing about two-thirds of their left wing of horse, . . . shogging also their foot and train much to the right, causing their right wing of horse to edge down towards the sea. We could not well imagine but that the enemy intended to attempt upon us, or to place themselves in a more exact condition of interposition. The Major-General [Lambert] and myself coming to the Earl Roxburgh's House, and observing this posture, I told him I thought it did give us an opportunity and advantage to attempt upon the enemy, to which he immediately replied, that he had thought to have said the same thing to me. . . . We called for Colonel Monk, and showed him the thing; and coming to our quarters at night, and demonstrating our apprehensions to some of the colonels, they also cheerfully concurred.

Captain John Hodgson, who describes this council of war, which took place about nine o'clock, shows that in fact not all the colonels were so cheerful. Many 'were for shipping the foot', and leaving the horse to attempt to force their passage to Berwick, but 'honest Lambert was against them'. He encouraged the rest to fight, pointing out that it would be daylight before they could embark the infantry and that all the carriages would be lost. Tactically the English had the advantage because they had only to beat Leslie's right wing, to put his whole army into confusion. Moreover, the Scots had left intervals between their bodies 'upon the brink of the hill', through which Cromwell's horse would be able to march a troop at a time, while the enemy would not be able to wheel about, or oppose them, without putting themselves into disorder. Lastly, the guns would 'have fair play' at Leslie's left wing, while the main body was attacking his right.

The night was very rainy and tempestuous. The English had cover in the town and their tents, but the Scots were still standing to their arms in the fields, where they were twice alarmed, though whether by accident or design does not appear. Towards morning the Commissioners suggested that they might take some rest, and orders were given to put out all matches but two in each company. And so, thinking themselves perfectly safe, the Scots made themselves shelters of the new reaped corn, and went to sleep. Some of the cavalry went foraging, and many unsaddled their horses. Many of the officers did not stay with their regiments, but sought cover from the rain.

Meanwhile, the sound of their movements deadened by the storm, the English were making ready. All night Cromwell, mounted on a little Scots nag, rode by torchlight through the various regiments 'biting his lips till the blood ran down his chin without his perceiving it, his thoughts being busily employed to be ready for the action now in hand'.

His plan was for six regiments of horse, and three and a half of foot to march in the van; Fleetwood, Lambert, Whalley and Monck were 'to lead on the business'. The foot brigades of Pride and Overton and the other two regiments of horse were to bring up the rear with the cannon. The 'time of falling-on' was to be break of day, sunrise being 5.33 a.m., but, owing to delays, it was not until six o'clock in the morning that they moved forward. Despite doubts and delays, Oliver, as before Naseby, was now in a mood of elation, in the words of an eyewitness '. . . carried on as with a divine impulse. He did laugh so excessively as if he had been drunk, and his eyes sparkled with spirits' (Aubrey).

The Scots field-word was *The Covenant*; the English *The Lord of Hosts*. Four cavalry regiments began the onset, the enemy cavalry being supported by foot and guns in a very good position to receive them. Cromwell writes: 'Before our foot could come up, the enemy made a gallant resistance, and there was a very hot dispute at the sword's point between our horse and theirs'. The first of the English infantry to get into action were overpowered and repulsed, but soon rallied.

> But my own regiment (of foot) under the command of Lieutenant-Colonel Goffe and my Major White, did come seasonably in; and, at the push of pike, did repel the stoutest regiment the enemy had there [the Highlanders of Lawers], merely with the courage the Lord was pleased

to give, which proved a great amazement to the residue of their foot. . . . The horse in the meantime did with a great deal of courage and spirit, beat back all opposition, charging through the bodies of the enemy's horse and their foot; who were, after the first repulse given, made by the Lord of Hosts as stubble to their swords . . .

Hodgson describes the last phase of the battle:

The General himself comes in the rear of our regiment, and commands [us] to incline to the left; that was to take more ground, to be clear of all bodies: and we did so, and horse and foot were engaged all over the field; and the Scots all in confusion: And, the sun appearing upon the sea, I heard Noll say, 'Now let God arise, and his enemies shall be scattered' [Psalm 68]; and he following us as we slowly marched, I heard him say, 'I profess they run!' [Hodgson goes on to explain that the Scots] routed one another, after we had done their work on their right wing; and we, coming up to the top of the [Doon] hill with the straggling parties, that had been engaged, kept them from bodying; and so the foot threw down their arms, and fled towards Dunbar, our pin-fold, and there they were surrounded and taken. The horse fled what way they could get, ours pursued towards Haddington; and the General made a halt, and sung the hundred and seventeenth psalm;

> O give you praise unto the Lord,
> All nations that be;
> Likewise you people all accord
> His name to magnify.
>
> For great to us-ward ever are
> His loving-kindnesses;
> His truth endures for evermore:
> The Lord O do ye bless.

By the time the psalm was done Cromwell's party had increased and was ready to advance '. . . the Scots ran, and were no more heard of that fight' (Hodgson).

In less than an hour, the best of the Scottish troops had been broken through and through and their whole army thrown into confusion, the defeat became a total rout, 'our men having the chase and execution of them near eight miles'.

Thus an army of 11,000 utterly defeated one of about 20,000. Cromwell estimated that 3,000 of the Scots were killed and 10,000 taken, besides some 30 guns, 200 colours and 15,000 arms. That the victors' losses should have been much less is only to be expected, though once more Cromwell's own estimate is scarcely credible: 'we lost not above thirty men' he wrote to Ireton. Never before had he fought against such odds and never had he displayed such tactical skill; well might he write: 'This is the Lord's doing, and it is marvellous in our eyes'.

Leslie too saw the result of the battle as 'the visible hand of God', though in some measure attributing his defeat to the laziness of his men who had neglected his orders to stand to their arms on the previous night.

To both sides the battle seemed a trial in which the Lord would judge between them. On 3 August, in a letter to the General Assembly of the Kirk of Scotland, Cromwell had used the famous argument: 'Is it therefore infallibly agreeable to the Word of God, all that you say? I beseech you, in the bowels of Christ, think it possible you may be mistaken'. When shortage of provisions had compelled him to withdraw from Musselburgh, on the 5th, the covenanting ministers had preached from the text 'The wicked flee when no man pursueth', but now the tables were turned with a vengeance. When Cromwell wrote to Hesilrige after the battle 'Surely it's probable the Kirk has done their do, I believe their King will set up upon his own score now', he showed himself a true prophet. The Covenanters were stunned by this 'dreadful appearance of God . . . after so many public appeals to him'. The Presbyterians could no longer hope to inflict their intolerant doctrines on Englishmen. The policy of the Solemn League and Covenant of 1644 was done with for ever.

Dunbar, fought against odds when the strategic position looked black, was Cromwell's greatest tactical victory. Lambert certainly seems to have made the running in the Council of War, but the responsibility was Cromwell's. His achievement was the more remarkable for he was beginning to feel his years, as he wrote to his wife next day: 'I have been in my inward man marvellously supported; though I assure thee, I grow an old man, and feel infirmities of age marvellously stealing upon me'.

After Dunbar Cromwell advanced and reduced Edinburgh and the west.

On 1 January Charles II was crowned at Scone so that he was now King in fact as well as name.

A serious illness, brought on by exposure, prevented Cromwell from taking the field before June 1651. Then he found Leslie strongly posted in the hills south of Stirling. He turned the position by sending Lambert with 4,000 men across the Forth into Fifeshire, where he defeated Sir John Brown at Inverkeithing on 20 July. Cromwell followed with more troops, and took Perth on 2 August, cutting Leslie's communications with the north, but leaving the way to England open. This bold strategy he justifies in a letter of 4 August to Lenthall:

> . . . we have done to the best of our judgments, knowing that if some issue were not put into this business, it would occasion another winter's war, to the ruin of your soldiery, for whom the Scots are too hard in respect of enduring the winter difficulties of this country, . . . but how to remove him out of this place, without doing what we have done, unless we had had a commanding army on both sides of the river of Forth, is not clear to us . . .

King Charles II, with the Scottish Royalists and Presbyterians now combined in his support, and hoping for substantial aid from the English Cavaliers, accepted the challenge.

20 Medal to commemorate the Victory at Dunbar

13   WORCESTER

It is, for aught I know, a crowning mercy.

CROMWELL's last campaign was to take little more than a month. He outlined his strategy on 4 August in a letter to Lenthall, and on 3 September, at Worcester, he destroyed the Scots army. In Scotland, for lack of troops, he had been unable to force a decision, but in England he could call upon all the home forces, both regular and militia, and thus achieve an overwhelming superiority.

Closely followed by Lambert and Harrison, the King, advancing down the western invasion route, was unable to thrust at the capital. Harried, and exhausted by the tedious march, he was glad to throw his army into the loyal city of Worcester (22 August) and there to await the crisis. The English Royalists, who looked upon the Scots as little, if any, better than Noll and his Roundheads, appeared in no great numbers, and Cromwell was able to cast his net about his stationary opponent at his leisure.

By 27 August Cromwell had concentrated 28,000 men at Evesham, and 5,000 militia at Coventry. To oppose this great host the King had perhaps 12,000 men, not more than 2,000 being English. Desertions and 'purple fever' had thinned his ranks. Although Cromwell's army was not so homogeneous as that which won Dunbar, its core was the pick of the army that had fought in Scotland. In point of morale too, the English had the advantage. Cromwell's men no more expected to be beaten than did the 8th Army which Montgomery took to Sicily. The Scots felt, in Hamilton's words, that they had 'one stout argument, despair'. Leslie, his nerve broken by Dunbar, was no commander for a desperate venture. He told the King that he was 'melancholic indeed, for he well knew that army, how well soever it looked, would not fight'. Though he proved wrong, it was to Charles's credit rather than his.

And while Leslie was proving infirm of purpose, Cromwell's strategy was never surer. On 28 August he sent Lambert to drive Massey from Upton-on-Severn. The Royalists were surprised and their commander wounded. Lambert set about repairing the bridge.

On the same day Oliver, whose men had been on the march since 6 August with but one day's rest, set up his headquarters at Spetchley (two miles south-east of Worcester), with the detachment under his immediate command astride the road to London.

On the 29th Cromwell wrote to Lenthall:

> . . . we know not yet which way the enemy will draw, our intelligence tells us that he is yet at Worcester, . . . We are this morn advancing towards that city: and I suppose we shall draw very close to it. If they will come forth and engage with us we shall leave the issue to God's providence, and doubt not to partake of glorious mercies. If they avoid fighting, and lead us a jaunt, we shall do as God shall direct, . . . The enemy hath raised a fort on this side the town, and burnt down divers out-houses.

The repairing of Fort Royal, a work erected in the First Civil War, was an indication that the Royalists had no intention of quitting Worcester. This simplified Cromwell's problem. To kill the war dead at a stroke he must destroy the King's army. While it lay at Worcester he could close in gradually, having superior numbers, and cut every avenue of escape.

On 29 August Cromwell occupied Perry Wood on the low ridge a mile east of the city, and opened fire with his big guns. Lilburne meanwhile was posted at Bewdley Bridge, and additional forces were raised in Lancashire in case the Scots should decide to retreat. In the Royalist camp the Council of War debated whether to march on London—now practically impossible—slip away into Wales, or bring in provisions and stay where they were. The cavalry thought of cutting their way out and making for Scotland, but were persuaded by the foot to stay. On the 31st a deserter reported that there was great distraction in the Scottish camp. Even so, on the night of 29 August they plucked up their courage and made a sortie from the east gate against the battery at Perry Wood. A Puritan tailor, one William Guise, betrayed the design, and though he swung for it next day, they were repulsed with loss. The English were in high spirits. Cromwell, riding to Upton on reconnaissance, 'was entertained with abundance of joy by extraordinary shouting from each regiment, troop, and company, as he went to salute them'. He had kept them busy gathering barges and planking for the construction of pontoon bridges. By 2 September all was ready.

The dawn of the anniversary of Dunbar found Cromwell at his command post, a cottage at the edge of Perry Wood. Fleetwood marched about five or six o'clock, but did not reach the Teme until the afternoon. Meanwhile, Cromwell had twenty great boats brought up to the junction of Severn and Teme, and a bridge was thrown across each river, the two being within pistol shot. It took some time to launch the bridges of boats, and by the time they were ready the Scots were in position.

King Charles from his splendid observation post, the cathedral tower, was watching the battle develop and deploying his out-numbered forces as best he could to counter Cromwell's moves. Major-General Montgomery and Sir William Keith were to hold Powick Bridge while Colonel Pitscotty, a veteran of Marston Moor, led 300 Highlanders to oppose the passage of the pontoons. Major-General Dalziel's brigade, deployed nearer Worcester, was to support these two forces.

With a splendid disregard for his responsibilities as Commander-in-Chief, Cromwell led the thrust across the Severn in person, being the first man to set foot on the west bank. His force, consisting of Hacker's regiment of horse, his own Lifeguard, Ingoldsby's and Fairfax's regiments of foot and part of his own regiment, followed shouting '*The Lord of Hosts!*'—their field-word at Dunbar. Major-General Deane led the column that crossed the Teme, and Pitscotty, resisting stubbornly, was slowly borne back from hedge to hedge by this flood of assailants.

Quitting the cathedral tower, the King galloped out to Powick Bridge and nerved his followers to a gallant resistance, but after a long fierce struggle the English forded the Teme and drove the Scots back into the St. John's suburb of Worcester.

The King still had one fresh force at his disposal, Leslie's cavalry drawn up in Pitchcroft, a great meadow north of the city. Seeing that Cromwell had committed the main body of his army west of the Severn, Charles resolved on a bold counterstroke. He would launch his reserve against the Parliamentarians on the east bank. And so it was that about sunset the Royalists came pouring out of St. Martin's and Sudbury Gates. The guns of Fort Royal thundered out in preparation for the attack, which was led by the King himself and the Duke of Hamilton. Scots and Cavaliers charged up the slopes of Red Hill, driving their enemies right back to their cannon before they were brought to a halt. The fight raged back and forth for three hours, but Lambert and Harrison hung on, and Cromwell had time to bring men back across the bridge of boats and turn the scale. After a desperate fight with pike and musket-butt, Charles's Highlanders, their ammunition spent, were swept back in the gathering darkness past Fort Royal and into the city. Never did Oliver expose himself more than in this, his last battle: 'My Lord General did exceedingly hazard himself, riding up and down in the midst of the shot and riding himself to the enemies' foot, offering them quarter, whereto they returned no answer but shot'.

The Royalists now retreated in much disorder through Sudbury Gate, the Essex militia stormed Fort Royal, put the garrison to the sword and turned the guns on the retreating Royalists. Meanwhile the Parliamentarians had possessed themselves of St. John's, where Dalziel's brigade craved quarter after a brief resistance. The fighting still raged in the streets of the city, where the English Cavaliers, led by the old Earl of Cleveland, made two gallant charges, gaining time for the young King to throw off his armour and escape. Some of the Scots resolutely maintained the Castle hill, eventually surrendering on quarter. The English Cavaliers made a last stand at the Town Hall, where, as a Royalist puts it: 'the rebels having in the end subdued all their opponents, fell to plundering the city unmercifully, few or none of the citizens escaping, but such as were of the fanatic party'.

Weary as he was, Oliver sat down at ten o'clock that night to pen a brief despatch to Lenthall:

> The enemy hath had great loss, and certainly is scattered, and run several ways. We are in pursuit of him, and have laid forces in several places, that we hope will gather him up.
>
> Indeed this hath been a very glorious mercy, and as stiff a contest, for four or five hours, as ever I have seen. Both your old forces and those new-raised have behaved themselves with very great courage . . .

This despatch he followed up next day with another in which he estimates the prisoners at 6,000 or 7,000, and his own losses at less than 200 men, probably an understatement. All the Scots baggage and artillery had been taken. He gives details of his plans to exploit his victory:

> I believe they had not many more than one thousand horse in their body that fled; I believe we have near four thousand following, and interposing between them and home; what fish they will catch, time will declare. . . . The dimensions of this mercy are above my thoughts. It is, for aught I know, a crowning mercy.

Cromwell had taken his measures with commendable foresight, and few indeed of the invaders escaped his net. There was one notable exception—the King, who in the only battle where he exercised supreme command showed himself a bold and enterprising commander. His dramatic escape owed almost as much to his own unshakable nerve and invincible sense of humour as to the loyalty of his subjects. Everything was against him. There was a price of £1,000 on his head, and being 'above two yards high', he was not a man to disappear readily into the background. But to Cromwell this escape was a blessing in disguise. With the blood of one King on his hands he may have been glad to be spared the 'cruel necessity' of sending his son to the scaffold, and increasing the gulf between himself and the old Royalists.

Worcester was both the crown and the end of Cromwell's military career, a splendid victory which did far more than foil an invasion. By depriving Scotland of her last field army it robbed that country of her independence. Monck's 6,000 veterans made short work of all resistance north of the border, and despite Glencairn's rising in 1653, the Cromwellian régime in Scotland was not to be upset while Oliver lived. If the English occupation left no indelible marks on that country, at least Burnet could write: 'we always reckon those eight years of usurpation as a time of great peace and prosperity'.

Worcester, the last great battle of the Civil Wars, was perhaps Cromwell's finest military achievement. And it was indeed to prove for him 'a crowning mercy'; though there were to be rebellions in the last seven years of his life, never again was he to see an enemy army on English soil.

Begone! It is time you should give way to honester men.

THERE were many who looked to the victor of Worcester, now that English republicans had at long last overthrown all their enemies, to bring about a glorious reformation in Church and State. But if Milton was soon to hail him as 'our chief of men', he was not himself ambitious to play the part either of Dictator or of King. In October the Tuscan ambassador wrote: 'there cannot be discovered in him any ambition save for the public good, to which he brings all his spirit and power'.

For his own part Oliver wrote at the same period: 'I am a poor weak creature . . . yet accepted to serve the Lord and his people. Indeed . . . you know not me, my weaknesses, my inordinate passions, my unskilfulness, and everyway unfitness to my work. Yet, yet the Lord, who will have mercy on whom He will, does as you see.' As Commander-in-Chief, member of Parliament and of the Council of State, Lord Lieutenant of Ireland and Chancellor of Oxford University, he had work enough without adding the rôle of national leader.

The actual government of the country at this time was being carried on by the Rump—the sixty or seventy members of the Long Parliament who still attended—whose abler members formed the Council of State, which managed the day-to-day administration of the country.

Soon after his return to London, Cromwell brought about a conference of officers and M.P.s to discuss the future government of the country. His own view, as stated in December 1651, was that 'a settlement with somewhat of monarchial power in it would be very effectual', though he was not thinking of the Restoration of the Stuarts. He was at one with the Army officers in wanting a new Parliament. But the members of the Long Parliament, with their own pecuniary interests in mind, were in no hurry to dissolve. Had they done anything to heal the wounds of the Civil War this might have been well enough, but they were far from bestirring themselves in that direction. It was not until February 1652 that Cromwell managed to induce them to pass an act of pardon for all treasons committed before Worcester, and even then the bill was so full of exceptions that it was practically worthless. Ludlow alleged that Cromwell was courting the Royalists to 'fortify himself by the addition of new friends for the carrying on his designs', but clearly it was no more than common sense and common justice to grant some sort of amnesty to the defeated Royalists.

The settlement of the Church seemed equally desirable. The Long Parliament had abolished Episcopacy without establishing anything in its place. The Rev. John Owen, formerly Cromwell's chaplain in Ireland, set himself the task of bringing order out of chaos. On 10 February 1652 he and a number of other ministers produced a comprehensive scheme, which the House of Commons referred to a Committee, whose most important member was Oliver. There was to be a national Church, but dissenters would be tolerated. Commissioners were to ensure the fitness of candidates wishing to be preachers, and were to eject unworthy ministers, or schoolmasters. Opponents of the fifteen fundamentals of Christianity were not to be permitted to propagate their views. This was too narrow for Cromwell's taste: 'I had rather', quoth he, 'that Mahometanism were permitted amongst us, than that one of God's children should be persecuted', an attitude which inspired the great Puritan poet's 'Ode to the Lord General Cromwell'.

> Cromwell, our chief of men, who through a cloud
> Not of war only, but detractions rude,
> Guided by faith and matchless fortitude,
> To peace and truth thy glorious way has ploughed,
> And on the neck of crownèd Fortune proud
> Has reared God's trophies, and his work pursued,
> . . . . : yet much remains
> To conquer still; Peace hath her victories
> No less renowned than War: new foes arise
> Threatening to bind our souls with secular chains,
> Help us to save free conscience from the paw
> Of hireling wolves, whose Gospel is their maw.

Cromwell, like Milton, was for allowing complete religious liberty—at least to 'the godly'—and in this he had the full support of the Army. Parliament, however, postponed any decision on the proposals of Cromwell's committee, for its attentions were now fully occupied by a new war. This time the enemy was not the Cavaliers, but one of the few foreign countries that had supported the rebels in their struggle against King Charles; the United Provinces.

Foreign affairs now began to engross Oliver's attention for the first time. In the spring of 1652 he had carried on a secret, but abortive, negotiation with Cardinal Mazarin in the hope that France might cede Dunkirk rather than allow it to fall into the hands of the Spaniards, and in April he had 5,000 troops at Dover, ready to embark at a moment's notice. But the war with Holland was for the moment more important than relations with the greater powers, France and Spain. When in May 1652 a chance clash off Dover between Blake and Van Tromp had led to war with Holland, Cromwell, who was sent by Parliament to investigate the causes of the fight, felt that Blake had upheld the Commonwealth's sovereignty over the British Seas, but his heart was not in the quarrel. 'I do not like the war', he told the Dutch congregation in London; 'I will do everything in my power to bring about peace'. Holland was after all a Protestant power. The war was in truth an economic one— perhaps in that sense the first 'modern' war. The Dutch controlled the Baltic trade, the spice trade with the Indies and the herring fisheries of the North Sea. The Rump's Navigation Act, forbidding all imports which were not carried in ships belonging to their country of origin or in English vessels, was an attempt to break this stranglehold.

The war went well at first, for England had the larger Navy and at the same time had less commerce to defend. But in November 1652 Van Tromp beat Blake off Dungeness, and wrested the command of the Channel from him for a space. The Baltic was closed to English trade; Denmark was on the point of joining the Dutch. In the Mediterranean the British squadrons were defeated or blockaded.

At home things looked black for the Commonwealth as 1652 drew to an end. The crippling cost of the war was met in part by confiscating the estates of Royalists. This odious measure provoked Cromwell's righteous wrath: 'Poor men', he said, 'were driven like flocks of sheep by forty in a morning to confiscation of goods and estates, without any man being able to give a reason why two of them should forfeit a shilling'.

In the Army discontent was rife. In August the council of officers petitioned Parliament to carry out a number of reforms—the old question of arrears raised its head once more. Fair words were to be had in plenty, but nothing was done. The Army became convinced that the members were a self-seeking body of 'profiteers'. 'My lord,' Cromwell told Whitelocke, 'there is little hope of a good settlement to be made by them, really there is not'. In his memoirs Whitelocke asserts that at this interview Oliver asked him: 'What if a man should take it upon himself to be King?' To this Whitelocke replied that it would be better to restore Charles II. Cromwell succeeded in curbing the discontent of his hot-headed followers until January 1653, when their impatience for a dissolution became practically uncontrollable. The House took alarm, and at long last began to consider the 'Bill for a New Representative' in good earnest. By mid-April the bill only needed a third reading, but in the meanwhile it had become modified so that the present members would keep their seats, merely recruiting their numbers.

'We should have had fine work then', said Cromwell. 'A Parliament of four hundred men, executing arbitrary government without intermission, except some change of a part of them; one Parliament stepping into the seat of another, just left warm for them; the same day that one left, the other was to leap in . . . I thought, and I think still, that this was a pitiful remedy.' The officers were not going to have this at any price. If they had been 'fought out of' their liberties and rights in the war, necessity would have taught them patience, 'but to deliver them up would render us the basest persons in the world, and worthy to be accounted haters of God and His people'. Lambert and Harrison urged Cromwell to dissolve the Rump by force, but still he hesitated. 'I am pushed on by two parties to do that, the consideration of the issue whereof makes my hair stand on end.'

There followed a conference between officers and members on 19 April 1653. It was suggested that the bill should be dropped, Parliament dissolved, and a provisional government appointed as had been done before when the land 'was under the like hurlyburlies'. The members reluctantly agreed to think it over and confer again the following day, Vane and others pledging themselves to suspend the bill meanwhile. When the House met next day, Hesilrige, who carried just as much weight as Vane, had arrived from the country.

He was determined to push the bill through, and carried the House with him. It was intended to choose a new general in place of Cromwell and to adjourn until November, leaving the Council of State to govern the country.

Major-General Harrison quickly sent news of these proceedings to Whitehall, and though at first Oliver would not believe 'that such persons would be so unworthy', further messages convinced him of the danger and he hurried down to the House. He took the precaution of leaving a body of thirty or forty musketeers from his own regiment in the lobby. For perhaps a quarter of an hour Oliver sat silent in his place. Then the Speaker put the question that 'this Bill do pass'. Cromwell whispered to Harrison: 'This is the time I must do it,' and, rising in his place, took off his hat, and began to speak. At first he praised the Parliament for the pains and care for the public good which had been characteristic of it in its early days, but he went on to reproach the members for their recent misdeeds, scorning 'their injustice, delays of justice, self-interest, and other faults . . . charging them not to have a heart to do anything for public good,' and to have 'espoused the corrupt interest of Presbytery and lawyers who were the supporters of tyranny and oppression'. His passion mounted as he spoke. 'Perhaps you think this is not Parliamentary language', he cried. 'I confess it is not, neither are you to expect any such from me.' Then he clapped his hat on his head, and began striding up and down the centre of the House, rebuking individuals as his eye lit upon them, while their fellows, it seems, looked on hypnotized.

'It is not fit that you should sit as a Parliament any longer. You have sat long enough, unless you had done more good.' This outburst at last produced an ineffectual protest from Sir Peter Wentworth. 'Come, come!' cried Oliver, 'I will put an end to your prating. You are no Parliament. I say you are no Parliament. I will put an end to your sitting.' On this he gave the order to Harrison: 'Call them in; call them in', the doors were flung open, and in came his musketeers.

When Vane protested: 'This is not honest, yea it is against morality and common honesty', Cromwell turned on him, saying more in sorrow than in anger, 'O, Sir Henry Vane! Sir Henry Vane! The Lord deliver me from Sir Henry Vane!'

Cromwell next pointed to the Speaker and cried 'Fetch him down'. But Lenthall showed himself as obstinate as he had been on an equally famous occasion when confronted by his King. Seeing that he refused to move without compulsion, Harrison intervened, saying, 'Sir, I will lend you my hand', and led him from his chair. Algernon Sidney offered some resistance, and Cromwell cried 'Put him out'. Harrison and another officer laid their hands on his shoulders and impelled him towards the door.

Cromwell's eye now lit upon the mace. 'What shall we do with this bauble?' he exclaimed, and then, calling to one of his captains: 'Here, take it away'. As the last of the fifty odd members departed, Cromwell called after them: 'It is you that have forced me to this, for I have sought the Lord night and day, that He would rather slay me than put me upon the doing this work'.

15   THE RELUCTANT DICTATOR, 1653–1655

. . . The Saints are marching on . . .

NONE but the ejected members mourned the dissolution of the Rump. 'There was not so much as the barking of a dog or any general and visible repining at it', said Cromwell afterwards. Since, during the afternoon, he had also dissolved the Council of State, the Commander-in-Chief was now the only remaining constituted authority. He was indeed dictator.

But if he found himself dictator, he was a reluctant one. He had not turned out the Rump to put the Army in its place. His action was not intended as an attack on Parliament as an institution. Quite the contrary. The Rump's very unworthiness of the name of a Parliament had tried his temper so that, after many months of hesitation, it had exploded and brought the session to its violent and unseemly end. The Army, though as anxious as its master to find a solution to the constitutional problem, was divided as to the best method. Lambert wished to leave power in the hands of a small council assisted by an elected Parliament. Harrison and the Fifth-Monarchy-Men were for replacing both Parliament and Council with a 'Sanhedrin' of seventy members.

Cromwell for his part felt that some kind of Parliament would be the body most acceptable to the country. A compromise was reached, which produced the assembly known as The Barebone Parliament.[1] It was a nominated body of 140 Puritan notables, 'men fearing God and hating covetousness'; its members were summoned individually by Cromwell as Captain-General. This was practically the solution put forward by the fanatical Harrison, under whose influence Oliver had now fallen. Harrison was very much 'a plain russet-coated captain'. A man of little education, he had shown himself a gallant fighter in many a desperate action. He was an Ironside of the 1644 vintage—those who had 'seen visions and had revelations'. Ireton, to whom Cromwell had so often turned in moments of perplexity, had died in Ireland in 1651, which partly accounts for Harrison's brief ascendancy.

The new Parliament met at Westminster on 4 July, and was welcomed by Cromwell who, in a long speech full of Scriptural quotations, told them of his pleasure that the government should at last have been entrusted to the godly. He had felt bound 'not to grasp at the power' himself, nor did he desire 'to keep it in military hands, no not for a day'. The time was not ripe for an elected Parliament, though, he protested: 'None can desire it more than I'. They must convince the nation 'that as men fearing God have fought them out of their bondage, so men fearing God do now rule them in the fear of God'. Neither the overthrow of the monarchy nor the dissolution of the Rump had come to pass by his design;

> I never looked to see such a day as this . . . Indeed it is marvellous, and it hath been unprojected. . . . And indeed this hath been the way God hath dealt with us all along; to keep things from our eyes . . . so that we have seen nothing in all His dispensations long beforehand—which is also a witness, in some measure, to our integrity.

This Assembly of Saints set to work full of optimism and zeal. It voted itself the title of Parliament—which its authors probably did

---

[1] So called after one of its members, Thomas, alias 'Praise-God', Barbon.

not intend for it—elected a new Council of State, and set up twelve committees to redress every sort of grievance. Its reforming zeal was all-embracing. Twenty-six Acts were passed between July and December. A single day's debate sufficed to do away with the Court of Chancery. Tithes and patronage were to be swept away, and a voluntary Church system was to be set up, though Cromwell managed to obstruct this. Because he still favoured a State Church he found himself denounced by both Anabaptist and Fifth-Monarchy preachers as 'the Old Dragon' and 'the Man of Sin'.

It was soon brought home to Oliver that few indeed of the assembly were as moderate as he. 'Fain would I have my service accepted of the Saints', he told his son-in-law, Major-General Fleetwood, 'if the Lord will, but it is not so. Being of different judgments, and those of each sort seeking most to propagate their own, that spirit of kindness that is to all, is hardly accepted of any'. The fanatics had got the bit between their teeth.

> The Lord begins to honour us,
> The Saints are marching on,
> The sword is sharp, the arrows swift
> To destroy Babylon.

The Fifth-Monarchy-Men were now thinking of making Harrison Lord General in place of Cromwell, so that by September the latter was beginning once more to listen to Lambert.

Lambert, besides being a brave and efficient soldier, was a genial but hard-headed Yorkshireman. He had a good opinion of his own abilities, could keep his counsel, was extremely ambitious and had a considerable talent for intrigue. He and some of the leading officers had now drawn up a written constitution, 'The Instrument of Government', embodying an elected legislative assembly. The executive power and the title of King were to be conferred upon Cromwell, but, while in the main he approved of their scheme, Oliver would not accept the royal title.

On 12 December these more moderate reformers relieved Cromwell of his Assembly of Saints by the simple device of getting up early and voting that Parliament should resign its powers into the hands of the Lord General, before the extremists could rally their full strength. This done, some eighty of them went in procession to

Whitehall and informed Cromwell of their action. About twenty-seven members, who kept their seats, were quickly dispersed by two files of musketeers.

Cromwell may well have had no foreknowledge of the stratagem which brought about the dissolution of the Barebone Parliament. He told the first Parliament of the Protectorate: 'I can say it in the presence of divers persons here who know whether I lie, that I did not know one tittle of that resignation, till they all came and brought it, and delivered it into my hands'. Though no man gave him the lie, he was glad enough—as in the case of Pride's Purge—to accept the *fait accompli*.

The dictator was now back where he had been when he dissolved the Rump: 'My power was again by this resignation as boundless and unlimited as before, all things being subject to arbitrariness, and myself a person having power over the three nations without bound or limit set; . . .' His experiment had failed. In after years he was to call it 'a story of my own weakness and folly'. 'And yet', he continued, 'it was done in my simplicity.' He had thought that 'men of our own judgment, who had fought in the wars', would work with him in harmony, 'and this was the naked truth, that the issue was not answerable to the simplicity and honesty of the design'.

Lambert now revived his rejected constitution, replacing the title of King by that of Protector. After several days' debate, Cromwell accepted, and on 16 December 1653, wearing a plain black coat in token that he was now a civilian not a soldier, he was installed as Protector. Accepting the new constitution, he said:

> I do promise in the presence of God that I will not violate or infringe the matters and things contained therein; but, to my power, observe the same, and cause them to be observed; and shall in all other things, to the best of my understanding, govern these nations according to the laws, statutes, and customs thereof; seeking their peace, and causing justice and law to be equally administered.

Harassed by Royalist and Leveller, and saddled with a foreign war of his own making, he was to prove incapable of living up to these good intentions. Nonetheless, this was not the language of a Hitler or a Mussolini.

It is hardly to be wondered at that the situation of the Commonwealth had not improved during the Barebone Parliament. The Dutch War still dragged on. At home the Levellers were giving trouble. Lilburne, banished in 1649, had reappeared in London and had been put on trial. The mob greeted his acquittal with a shout that could be heard a mile off, while the soldiers guarding the court showed their sympathy by beating their drums. In the Highlands Glencairn was in arms, while nearer home the Cavaliers, quiet since Worcester, began to wonder whether the revolution had not shot its bolt. During the summer of 1653 plots to seize Poole and Portsmouth had been discovered.

Clearly the first task of Oliver's new government was to secure peace. Within four months of becoming Protector he had concluded a treaty with the Dutch, by which they admitted the supremacy of the British flag in British waters, renounced their support of the Royalists, and gave up their demands for the modification of the Navigation Act. This treaty was signed on 5 April 1654, and Cromwell gave a banquet to the Dutch Ambassadors, at which all present sang the 123rd Psalm together: 'Behold how good and how pleasant it is for brethren to dwell together in unity'. This was a good start, for it ended a war with a Protestant power, protected British commerce, and rendered less likely a Restoration of the Stuarts by foreign aid. But the terms were still stiff enough to be resented by the majority of the Dutch people, and Oliver's hopes for a league with the United Provinces were doomed to disappointment, for the commercial rivalry of the two powers remained unabated.

A state of war, though undeclared, existed between England and France, for Cardinal Mazarin had never recognized the Commonwealth. The establishment of the Protectorate, however, brought about a vast improvement in the climate of foreign affairs. Both France and Spain, which had been at war with each other for some years, now began to compete for an alliance with England, desiring the support of the strongest naval power in Europe.

The majority of the council favoured the French alliance, though a minority, headed by Lambert, preferred that of Spain. Oliver, slow as ever to make up his mind when he had no preconceived ideas on a subject, did not commit himself. He had good reason to be cau-

tious. Though the end of the Dutch War had released Monck for
duty in Scotland—he had been serving as an admiral—it would take
time even for so able an officer to suppress Glencairn's rising. Moreover, the resources of the Commonwealth were so limited that its
rulers would have done well to eschew all thought of further wars.
But with the two strongest military powers neutralising each other's
forces, the temptation to intervene was very strong.

During the summer of 1654 elections were held, as promised by
the 'Instrument', and the first Parliament of the Protectorate
gathered at Westminster. At least a hundred of the members had sat
in the Long Parliament. Despite the government's powers of elec-
toral manipulation, there were some forty Presbyterians who had
not been seen since Pride's Purge. Hesilrige was back, and there
were a number of other republicans: men who regarded the Protector as a traitor to the 'good old cause'. Wildman the Leveller had
been elected but forbidden by the Council to take his seat. Wales
and the West had even ventured to send a few Royalists to Westminster. Even so, Cromwell's supporters, Army officers for the most
part, certainly outnumbered the potential opposition.

Major-General Lambert opened the proceedings by announcing
that Cromwell awaited the members in the Painted Chamber. The
Republican Bradshaw, who had presided at the trial of King Charles,
set up a cry of 'Sit still!', but nevertheless the members trooped off
to hear the Protector's words of welcome.

Next day Cromwell made a speech in which he called for healing
and settlement. He attacked the Levellers and the Fifth-Monarchy-
Men, and outlined the achievements of his government, assuring the
members that he was resolved to be 'a fellow servant' with them.
They were, he said, a free Parliament—and in this at least they were
agreed.

Parliament indeed lost no time in demonstrating its sense of its
own dignity. Lenthall, the Speaker of the Long Parliament, was re-
elected to that office. The Serjeant-at-Arms was ordered to bring
in the mace—'that bauble'. The next step was to claim the sovereign
powers enjoyed by the Long Parliament. 'The government, should
be in Parliament and a single person limited or restrained as the Parliament should think fit.' Cromwell was prepared to accept some
modification of the 'Instrument', but on four fundamental principles

he would not budge. There was to be government by a single person and Parliament; the control of the armed forces was to be divided between Parliament and Protector; the time for which a Parliament might sit was to be limited. Lastly there was to be liberty of conscience—at least for the 'godly'. Feeling that his power had been ratified by the nation, Oliver would not lightly surrender it: 'The wilful throwing away of this Government, so owned by God, so approved by men,—I can sooner be willing to be rolled into my grave and buried with infamy, than I can give my consent unto'.

A hundred members, including Hesilrige, refused to sign the Engagement to be faithful to Commonwealth and Protector, and were excluded. The rest set to work to revise the constitution, but there could be no truly constitutional government, when only the sword of the Protector kept the country from anarchy.

★   ★   ★

Meanwhile, the Protector, after wavering for some months, made up his mind on the major problem of foreign affairs. At first he had been resolved not to involve the Commonwealth in the European struggle, but to remain, if possible, on good terms with both France and Spain, but it was not to be. He desired, not unreasonably, that the Spaniards should abandon their long-standing hostility to English traders and colonists in the West Indies, and allow English merchants the free exercise of their religion. This was not well received by the Spanish Ambassador: 'To ask liberty from the Inquisition and free sailing in the West Indies', he said, 'was to ask for his master's two eyes'. Cromwell now determined (August 1654) to show his power by despatching an expedition to the West Indies, with orders not only to attack the Spanish colonies, but to capture such French ships as it should encounter. This was Elizabethan diplomacy with a vengeance, but Oliver, incredible though it may seem, did not believe that it would lead to war with the Spaniards in Europe.

The expedition was so ill-found that Cromwell's preparations have been compared with those of Buckingham for La Rochelle. Although at the end of 1654 the standing army numbered 57,000, as opposed to the 30,000 allowed by the Instrument, only 2,500 were allotted to the expedition which sailed from Portsmouth in December. Admiral Penn with thirty-eight sail made for the West Indies, where the General, Venables, raised some 4,500 more men at Barbados, St. Kitts and elsewhere. The men sent out from England were insufficient to leaven this mass of recruits, and when in April Venables landed in Hispaniola (San Domingo) he was ignominiously defeated. He re-embarked and sailed for Jamaica, which he occupied in May, though sickness soon decimated the force. Penn and Venables made matters worse by their quarrels, and when they returned to England the Protector lodged them in the Tower. 'The Lord hath greatly humbled us', said Cromwell, and took to his bed.

Nevertheless, he was resolved to hold on to what had been won by this ill-conceived expedition. Major-General Fortescue was promised supplies and reinforcements: 'it is much designed amongst us to strive with the Spaniards for the mastery of all those seas'. Recovering quickly from his first humiliation the Protector wrote to Vice-Admiral Goodwin with all his old fervour:

> Set up your banners in the name of Christ, for undoubtedly it is his cause. And let the reproach and shame that hath been for your sins, and through the misguidance of some, lift up your hearts to confidence in the Lord, and for the redemption of his honour from men who attribute their success to their idols, the work of their own hands . . .

They had to do with 'that Roman Babylon of which the Spaniard is the great underpropper. In this respect we fight the Lord's battles'.

And if the first news of the disaster in Hispaniola was a blow to the government, in the long run things turned out well enough. Jamaica was settled by people from St. Kitts, Barbados, Nevis and the Bermudas, and despite repeated attempts by the Spaniards survived, and survives as the chief fruit of Oliver's foreign policy, for Charles II was to compel Spain to recognize our right to retain it.

While the train of events he had set in motion was unfolding itself in the West Indies, things were coming to a head between the Protector and his first Parliament. On two points they could not agree. Firstly, the House was not prepared to allow the degree of religious liberty that Cromwell desired. Secondly, in its bid for sovereignty, the Parliament intended to reserve to itself financial control of the armed forces, upon which the Protector replied, 'If the power of the militia should be yielded up at such a time as this, when there is so much need of it to keep this cause, as there was to get it, what would become of us all?'

The Instrument had laid down that the House should sit for five months. On 22 January 1655 when precisely five lunar months had passed, Oliver showed that the last word still lay with him and the Army: 'I think it my duty to tell you that it is not for the profit of these nations, nor for common and public good for you to continue longer, and therefore I do declare unto you, that I do dissolve this Parliament'.

Oliver now intended that his rule should be based on the Instrument of Government, but he bargained without the Cavaliers. Already in May 1654 John Gerard's plot to assassinate the Protector had been uncovered, and had been followed by a wave of arrests, and the execution (10 July) of its author. A far more formidable attempt followed. By midsummer 1654 the Action party, which planned for nothing less than a general rising, had come into being. This time the Cavaliers hoped for support from Presbyterians, Levellers and discontented Army officers, but when the insurrection came in March 1655 it was a purely Royalist affair. Cromwell's government was vigilant, and he was fortunate in John Thurloe, the able civil servant who was Secretary to the Council. In the last weeks of 1654, this official gave warning of both Royalist and Leveller conspiracies, and military precautions were taken. Cromwell summoned troops from Ireland, concentrated regiments in London and increased the garrison of the Tower. In January Thurloe's agents discovered the Action party's organization for distributing arms in the Midlands, and a wave of arrests followed. Major Henry Norwood, who had been supplying the Cavaliers with weapons bought from London gunsmiths, was considered sufficiently important to be examined by Oliver in person, but as Thurloe records 'he proved a peremptory fellow, and would not confess'. Others proved less stouthearted, and more arrests resulted. On 13 February the Protector was able to give a personal exposition of both the Royalist and the Leveller plots to the Lord Mayor and Common Council of London. Further precautions followed: horses were confiscated, and private stores of powder; race meetings, under cover of which Royalists used to meet, were forbidden.

Although discouraged by the evident vigilance of the government, the Royalists persisted with their plan for simultaneous risings all over the country. After various postponements, 8 March was fixed upon as the day. Here and there bodies of horse collected, though most, like those who chose the ill-omened field of Marston Moor as their rendezvous, fled before dawn, 'strangely frightened with their own shadows'. For the most part the Cavaliers waited to see what good their comrades might do elsewhere, but in the West Country at least they managed to strike a blow.

Colonel John Penruddock, a Wiltshire gentleman, did not rise until 11 March, but when he did he surprised Salisbury, seized the High Sheriff and the judges of assize, and proclaimed King Charles II. The Royalists, 400 strong, now moved westwards, hoping to raise more men, but on 14 March they were attacked at South Molton by sixty horse from Exeter, and after a few hours' fighting surrendered on a promise of quarter. Penruddock and some of his followers were executed, the remainder being transported without legal trial to Barbados. The insurrection had been ill-co-ordinated, largely because of the difficulty of liaison between the various Royalist centres. Their security had not been good, and the vigilant Thurloe had been able to build up a picture of their activities, so that Cromwell could warn his garrisons and the militia, and move his forces where necessary. But owing to divisions in their leadership, the Royalists had been very far from deploying their full strength, nor had they enlisted the aid of the Presbyterian opposition. Despite their apparently easy victory, Cromwell and Thurloe were convinced by the mixture of fact and fiction that came from their various spies that there was more trouble ahead. In May it was reported from Cologne that a group of exiles were planning to assassinate the Protector with 'a stone-bow made after a very extraordinary manner' which 'would shoot a bullet of Carbine bigness about 40 yards with an incredible strength'.

In the summer of 1655 Cromwell felt strong enough to disband some 10,000 soldiers. This was the more necessary since the Commonwealth was in financial difficulties. In 1654 its revenue had been £2,250,000 while its expenditure had been £2,670,000 But while cutting down the strength of his standing force, he adopted a scheme for the policing of the kingdom, which though odious was at least reasonably successful. He divided the country into eleven districts and over each he set a Major-General. This measure was a direct result of the alarm caused by Penruddock's Rising.

21 Medal commemorating Blake's Victories

16   THE CONSTABLE, 1655–1658

> I am ready to serve not as a king, but as a constable . . . a good constable to keep the peace of the parish.

THE rising of 1655 convinced the Protector that his attempts to reconcile the Royalist party had failed. He denounced them as 'implacable in their malice and revenge and never to be drawn from their adhering to that cursed interest'. Nevertheless, a good number of Cavaliers, having compounded for their estates, had been content to live in peace. In the words of one of them:

> *From the first war I have not struck a stroke*
> *But from the camp betook me to my book.*
> *Though I confess I had an itching hand*
> *To work some feat, but I took no command.*

The measures which the Protector now took fell on all Royalists, regardless of whether they had participated in the recent rising or not. A discriminatory tax, the Decimation Tax, was now imposed upon all former Cavaliers, so as to pay for the troops of horse with which the major-generals policed their districts. Most of the Royalists submitted quietly to this monstrous imposition, though some, who had previously compounded, refused to pay on the grounds that they were exempted by that same Act of Oblivion which Cromwell himself had sponsored. Whalley, perhaps the most lenient of the major-generals, confined Sir John Monson to his house and quartered fifty soldiers on him for refusing to pay, threatening to send another 500 if he persisted. When Major-General Boteler, the most detested of all these 'gauleiters', told a delinquent that he would make him declare against Christ or eat his sword, the Protector declined to intervene. When he did show leniency, as he occasionally did in cases where the King's former adherents could prove that they had a change of heart, the military objected, fearing that this would weaken the authority of the major-generals and encourage sedition.

Yet more comprehensive anti-Royalist measures followed. All who had fought the Commonwealth were to give bonds for their peaceable behaviour and for that of their servants. It was left to the major-generals to fix the size of these securities. When the Earl of Southampton, who had compounded on Oxford Articles, declined to pay, he was sent to the Tower. Cromwell had denounced the Long Parliament for its treatment of the Cavaliers. Now, through his major-generals, he treated them worse than the Parliamentarians had done at any time since the beginning of the First Civil War. 'The Protector's Declaration of October 1655 formally renewed the division of the nation into two hostile factions, and to treat the party as irreconcilable was an infallible means of making it so' (Underdown).

The financial difficulties of Cromwell's government could not be solved by the decimations alone. Within a week of the capture of Penruddock, orders had been sent to Blake (19 March) to attack the Spanish treasure fleet on its homeward voyage from South America. In June he was ordered to prevent the Spaniards from reinforcing the West Indies where, as we have seen, Penn and Venables were operating. Cromwell intended that these two expeditions would not only bring the light of the Gospel into those parts, but would make him master of the gold mines of Peru. He was to be dis-appointed, and this attempt on her colonies was so ill-resented by Spain that she declared war. Oliver was surprised, but he certainly should not have been. The Spanish ambassador departed on 24 Octo-ber, and on the same day Cromwell signed a commercial treaty with France, which contained a secret clause for the expulsion of the leading Royalists. At the same time the French promised to respect the rights of the Huguenots.

Meanwhile, Oliver was negotiating with Sweden, hoping to form a general league of Protestant states. 'Bring us back a Protestant alli-ance', he had told his ambassador, Whitelocke, in 1654, and before the abdication of Queen Christina, a treaty had been signed (11 April 1654). But when in June 1655 King Charles Gustavus invaded Poland and sent an envoy to request men, money and ships, he found only fair words and good entertainment. 'They dine, sup, hunt, and play bowls together', and 'never was ambassador, or indeed any man, so much caressed and regarded by Cromwell as this man is . . .' The truth is, too many of Oliver's 160 ships were tied up in the West Indies for him to be able to send many to the Baltic. And how-ever much he would have liked to have struck a blow against Catho-lic Poland—'wresting a horn from the head of the Beast', he called it—he was afraid of becoming embroiled with the Dutch or the Danes, Sweden had to be content with a commercial treaty which was signed in July 1656.

During 1655 and 1656 the English fleet cruised off the coasts of Spain. Cromwell actually contemplated the seizure of Gibraltar, and wrote to Blake: 'If possessed and made tenable by us, would it not be an advantage to us and an annoyance to the Spaniards, and enable us, without keeping so great a fleet on that coast, with six nimble frigates lodged there to do the Spaniards more harm than by a fleet and ease our own charge?' If his great admiral did not concur it was because he had no landing force at his command. To antici-pate somewhat, Blake's blockade eventually met with some success, for on 8 September 1656, Captain Stayner defeated a Spanish squad-ron off Cadiz, taking a ship with a cargo worth £600,000, and on 20 April 1657 he sank or burnt a treasure fleet of 16 vessels under the guns of Santa Cruz de Tenerife without the loss of a single ship.

*   *   *

In the summer of 1656 the need for money to pay for his Spanish war reduced the Protector to calling a Parliament. By the terms of the Instrument he need not have done so until 1657, but the major-generals assured him that they could secure the election of members friendly to the government. They overrated their power to over-awe the electorate: so many opposition candidates were returned that the Council was reduced to excluding no fewer than a hundred as disaffected to the government. The survivors, moderate Presby-terians or Independents, were docile enough. Even so, Oliver was fortunate in that the news of Stayner's success came soon after the session began, and induced the House to vote £400,000 towards the expenses of the Spanish War.

Thereafter this Parliament, like his others, showed itself little in sympathy with the Protector's policies. In matters of religion he was too tolerant for its taste, as the case of James Naylor exemplifies. Naylor, an old soldier and an early disciple of Fox the Quaker, had been thrown into prison for blasphemy when he permitted his fol-lowers to hail him as a new Messiah. Parliament, usurping judicial powers, voted, after much debate that the poor misguided enthus-iast should be branded, whipped and imprisoned. It was only with difficulty that the Protector managed to save Naylor's life.

The House showed an equally independent spirit when—very rightly—it threw out the militia bill by which it was proposed to con-tinue the Decimation Tax, Cromwell's son-in-law, Claypole, being one of those who spoke against it. In this debate the major-generals were assailed from all sides. Such was the hostility to their rule that many dreaded its continuance more than they feared a Royalist rising. Cromwell himself was beginning to be out of sympathy with his officers, and in truth they were showing themselves indecently arrogant. When the question arose of indemnifying the major-generals for any illegalities they might have committed, they brag-ged that their swords would indemnify them.

These debates were still going on when another assassination plot was detected. Miles Sindercombe, a Leveller who had formerly served as a quartermaster, had spent the last two years in hatching various plots to kill the Protector when he was caught trying to set fire to the chapel of Whitehall with an incendiary machine. He had hoped in the ensuing confusion to get his chance to kill Cromwell.

Sentenced to death for high treason, he poisoned himself in the Tower (13 February 1657) and was mourned by the Levellers as one worthy 'to be registered with Brutus and Cato'. When the details of this plot were laid before Parliament, an address of congratulation was offered to the Protector. A little-known Presbyterian member, Mr. Ashe, proposed an addition: 'It would tend very much to the preservation of himself and us that his Highness would be pleased to take upon him the government according to the ancient constitution'. In the first draft of the 'Instrument of Government' Cromwell had been offered the title of King. Now the question arose once more.

Hostility to military rule was not only manifested in the rejection of the militia bill. It prompted the framing of a revised constitution known as 'The Humble Petition and Advice'. Its framers wished to replace the Instrument with a form of government more familiar to the English people, and in the opening clause they invited Oliver to assume the title and dignity of King. The major-generals, supported by the soldiers and the Republicans, stubbornly fought the bill, clause by clause, but on 25 March the House resolved by 123 votes to 62 that the Protector should be asked to become King. The scheme was presented to Cromwell on the 31st.

Oliver wavered. He approved the new constitution and was grateful for the honour done him, but nevertheless he declined it. He could not 'find it his duty to God and Parliament to undertake this charge under that title'. During the weeks that followed, committees of Parliament pressed the old regicide to change his mind. Ironically enough, nothing would do to satisfy these erstwhile rebels but the title of King. As Thurloe put it:

> Parliament will not be persuaded that there can be a settlement any other way. The title is not the question, but it's the office, which is known to the laws and to the people. They know their duty to a King and his to them. Whatever else there is will be wholly new, and upon the next occasion will be changed again. Besides they say the name Protector came in with the sword, and will never be the ground of any settlement, nor will there be a free Parliament so long as that continues, and as it savours of the sword now, so it will at last bring all things to be military.

Thus his ablest civil servant laid bare the shallow foundations on which Oliver had tried in vain to build. But though his rule had all along depended on the Army the Protector was anxious to rule constitutionally, and by the consent of the nation. He was not greatly interested in the forms of government, but he thought the new constitution would serve: 'The things provided in the Petition do secure the liberties of the people of God so as they never before had them.' But if he was 'hugely taken with the thing', the soldiers considered that his acceptance of the crown would be a 'fearful apostasy'. Petitioned by a hundred of them, led by Lambert, he had told them that he loved the title as little as they. It was but 'a feather in a hat'. At the same time he reminded them that 'Time was when they boggled not at the word King'. Had they not offered it to him in the first draft of the Instrument? Lambert, Fleetwood and Desborough brought pressure to bear by threatening to resign their commissions if he accepted, and on 8 May 1657 Cromwell finally refused Parliament: 'Though I think the act of government doth consist of very excellent parts in all but that one thing of the title as to me, I cannot undertake this government with the title of King'. Thus, as in so many political crises, in the end he went with the Army.

Parliament was content to accept his decision, for the long debates had shown his sympathy for their aims and on 25 May the Petition was once more presented, the title of Protector being substituted for that of King, and received his consent. On 26 June he was installed as Protector for the second time. The Speaker invested him in Westminster Hall with a robe of purple velvet, lined with ermine, 'The habit anciently used at the investiture of princes, presented him with a Bible and girt a sword to his side: then he placed a golden sceptre in his hands. Oliver took the oath to maintain the Protestant religion and preserve the peace and rights of the three nations, and seated himself upon the Royal Chair of Scotland. There followed a fanfare of trumpets and the people set up a cry of 'God save the Lord Protector!' Thereafter he was proclaimed by the heralds as Kings had been in times past.

The Venetian envoy compared the ceremony to a funeral, and no doubt the Protector himself thought all this pomp and ceremony 'foolery'; his golden sceptre a 'bauble', but, politically, he had had his way and was probably well content. His powers were greater than they had been under the Instrument. He had now the right not only to name his successor, but to appoint—with the approval of

Parliament—a Second Chamber. He was given a revenue of £1,300,000 per annum which was thought sufficient for the normal working of Government, and an addition of £600,000 for the next three years to pay for his Spanish war. At the same time Parliament also had gained ground. The arbitrary exclusion of its members, the device to which Oliver and his Council had habitually resorted, in order to ensure a subservient assembly, was no longer possible.

Thus far the war with Spain had been waged at sea and in the West Indies. But in April 1656 a treaty had been signed between Philip IV and Charles II which enabled the latter to maintain a small Royalist army in Flanders. On 23 March 1657 Cromwell signed an alliance with France by which he was to send 6,000 soldiers, supported by a fleet, to fight the Spaniards in Flanders. His share of the spoils was to be Mardyke and Dunkirk, which Thurloe thought would be a 'bridle to the Dutch, and a door into the continent'. Mardyke fell (3 October 1657) and was duly handed over, and Dunkirk was besieged the following year. In the battle of the Dunes (4 June 1658) the English redcoats won the admiration of friend and foe alike, storming the key of the enemy position, enabling Turenne to rout the Spaniards. Dunkirk fell ten days later, and at last Cromwell had his foothold on the Continent. But this is to anticipate a little.

In January 1658 the second Parliament of the Protectorate had met again after a six months' recess. In the interim the new Upper House had been selected. Cromwell could not risk making it very representative, and it included seven members of his family and seventeen regimental commanders. The republican view of this assembly is well-expressed by Mrs. Hutchinson, who says that Cromwell 'took upon himself to make lords and knights, and wanted not many fools, both of the army and gentry, to accept of and strut in this mock title'. Members of the old nobility and men of property were conspicuous by their absence.

The translation of Oliver's chief supporters to the Upper House left the 'opposition' in a strong position in the Commons, the more so since there was now no real obstacle to the return of diehard republicans, like Hesilrige. They had only to take an oath to be true and faithful to the Protector, and not to contrive anything against his lawful authority. This they did not scruple to do, yet they numbered

22 CROMWELL EXPELLING PARLIAMENT, 1653
From a contemporary Dutch print

23 'THE LORD PROTECTOR LYING IN STATE . . .'
From a contemporary print

24 THE GREAT SEAL OF THE COMMONWEALTH, 1651 (slightly reduced)
Designed by Thomas Simon

among them opponents of the Protectorate as determined as any Cavalier. Their feelings had never recovered from the wound they had suffered when Cromwell dissolved the Rump.

The Protector greeted this new assembly in the mood of hope and confidence which characterized him on such occasions, rejoicing 'How God hath redeemed us as we stand this day! Not from trouble and sorrow and anger only, but into a blessed and happy estate and condition comprehensive of all interests'. They had peace after ten years' war, and, after years of persecution, 'liberty to worship God without fear of enemies'. '... You shall be "the repairers of breaches, and the restorers of paths to dwell in"'. And if there be any higher work which mortals can attain unto in the world beyond this, I acknowledge my ignorance of it.'

His optimism was short-lived. In the Commons the Cromwellians, outnumbered now, lost the initiative at the outset, and days were spent debating whether the new second chamber was to be called 'the other House' or 'the House of Lords'. The republican leaders were determined to pull down the Protectorate, and were by no means content to vent their spleen in the House. They arranged for a petition, to be signed by 10,000 Londoners, to demand the limitation of the Protector's power over the Army, and the recognition of the House of Commons as the supreme authority. The House was to vote an address supporting these principles. They were ready, if need were, to make Fairfax commander-in-chief instead of Cromwell. Oliver's own regiment of horse was seething with discontent, and in consequence the republicans hoped for some backing from the Army. By a snap vote they intended to restore the republic and recall the Long Parliament.

Cromwell was not taken by surprise, as he had so nearly been on the day he dissolved the Rump. On 4 February 1658 he summoned both Houses to meet him, and told them he was Protector by virtue of the Humble Petition and Advice. 'There is not a man living can say I sought it, no, not a man nor woman treading upon English ground.' Instead of supporting this settlement, the Commons had striven to upset it. 'The nation is in likelihood of running into more confusion in these fifteen or sixteen days that you have sat, than it hath been from the rising of the last session to this day.' He denounced those who were trying to enlist the support of the Army and 'to stir up the people of this town into a tumulting'—'playing of the King of Scots' game' he called it. 'I think it high time that an end be put to your sitting, and I do dissolve this Parliament. And let God be judge between you and me.'

'Amen', retorted the unrepentant republicans.

Two days later Cromwell made a long speech to the senior officers of the Army explaining what he had done. Almost to a man they promised 'to stand and fall, live and die with my Lord Protector'. When Fleetwood had remonstrated with him over the dissolution, he had rebuked him, saying, 'You are a milksop; by the living God I will dissolve the House!' Certainly events now showed that he could still count on his old—one is tempted to say his *only*—supporters: the soldiery. Certainly the rupture shows that he had not the backing in the country to govern within the limits of a written constitution. Neither the Instrument nor the Humble Petition and Advice had served to conceal the fundamental fact that ultimately—whether he liked it or not—his rule was the rule of the sword.

And his sword was no longer the weapon of Naseby and Dunbar. He had broken with Harrison in 1654, with Lambert in 1657. And now his own regiment failed him. The Protector summoned the troop commanders, 'who all declared their dislike of the present government, and . . . seemed to speak of the goodness of a commonwealth'. The captains, though dissatisfied, were 'willing still to continue in the army and follow his Highness upon the grounds of the old cause, but would not express what they meant by the old cause'. The Protector dismissed the lot, including the commanding officer, Major William Packer, who later explained how he had lost his commission. He had thought Cromwell's second chamber

was not a 'Lords' House, but another House. But for my undertaking to judge this, I was sent for, accused of perjury, and outed of a place of £600 per annum. I would not give it up. He told me I was not apt: I, that had served him fourteen years, ever since he was captain of a troop of horse . . . and had commanded a regiment seven years: without any trial or appeal, with the breath of his nostrils I was outed; and lost not only my place, but a dear friend to boot. Five captains under my command, all of integrity, courage, and valour, were outed with me . . .

In mid-May 1658 there was an alarm. On the 15th the guards were doubled throughout London, and certain Royalists were arrested, the only prominent one being Sir William Leighton, who had fought at Naseby and Colchester. The plan, according to the government newspapers, had been to set fire to the City that night, to rout Colonel Pride's regiment in Southwark and to 'alarum' Whitehall. The French and Venetian envoys both thought this 'a put up job' to excite hatred against the Royalists at the time when Sir Henry Slingsby and other Royalists were to be tried for high treason.

Giavarina, the Venetian, wrote (24 May):

> It is true that the partisans of King Charles are constantly meditating some rising in the Kingdom, but it is also a fact that the Protector frequently causes conspiracies to spring up suddenly to give him an opportunity of imprisoning those whom he does not love . . . , and to display his vigilance . . . [and to induce the people] to obey him blindly and make the contributions in money which he is always demanding of them in the way of taxes.

Slingsby had been 'trepanned' by Cromwell and Thurloe. In December 1657 he had attempted to subvert Major Waterhouse, one of the garrison of Hull. The Major reported the matter, and was instructed to lead the Royalist on until there was legal proof of his treason, every stage of the operation being controlled by the Protector and his minion. Slingsby went to the block on 8 June, and was followed soon after by Dr. Hewitt, another conspirator.

The summer of 1658 was an unhealthy one. A malignant fever raged, and a day of public humiliation was ordered on account of it. On 6 August Cromwell's favourite daughter, Elizabeth Claypole, died at Hampton Court, apparently of cancer. It seems that as she lay dying she reproached her father for the death of Charles I and Dr. Hewitt. 'The sense of her outward misery in the pains she endured, took deep impression upon him, who indeed ever was a most indulgent and tender Father . . .' His own health had been undermined by long campaigning; he had been dangerously ill both in 1648 and 1651. He was ill before his daughter's death; attendance on her made matters worse: he was too ill to attend her funeral and in August he himself took to his bed. His illness was diagnosed as 'a bastard tertian ague', presumably a fever akin to malaria. George Fox, the Quaker, saw him on 20 August:

> I met him riding into Hampton Court Park, and before I came at him, he was riding in the head of his lifeguard, and I saw and felt a waft of

death go forth against him, that he looked like a dead man, and when I had spoken to him of the sufferings of Friends and warned him as I was moved to speak to him he bid me come to his house . . .

Next day Fox went up to Hampton Court, and was told that the Protector was very sick and that the doctors were not willing to let him speak with him. The fever worsened, and the Protector moved to London for a change of air. 'I shall not die this bout, I am sure on't', he told his wife, but the fever was too strong for him. 'It is a fearful thing to fall into the hands of the living God', he muttered, but towards the end he became clear in his mind and peaceful.

'The Lord hath filled me with as much assurance of His pardon and His love as my soul can hold . . . I am the poorest wretch that lives, but I love God, or rather am beloved of God.' On the afternoon of 3 September, the anniversary of Dunbar and Worcester, and the day after a great tempest, he died. The Protector's body was embalmed, and so elaborate were the arrangements that the funeral did not take place until 23 November. He was buried 'amongst kings and with a more than regal solemnity' in Henry VII's chapel in Westminster Abbey. The funeral cost £60,000—of which £19,000 were still owing in 1659. One cannot believe that Cromwell—or his thrifty wife—would have wished for such pomp.

Evelyn, a Royalist, recorded that the soldiers marched along in disorderly fashion, smoking as they went. It was, he said, 'the joyfullest funeral I ever saw, for there were none that cried but dogs'.

17   CROMWELL AS SOLDIER AND STATESMAN

. . . Peace hath her victories no less renown'd than War . . .

CROMWELL'S great military victories were not equalled by any achievements in the political field.

He was the most successful military commander on either side during the Civil Wars. It is idle to compare him with the great

British generals of other periods, for the numbers employed and the techniques of war were very different. Suffice it to say that he was not quite in the same class as Marlborough, Wellington and the great commanders of the Second World War. His military career was nevertheless phenomenal. With no previous military training he began his soldiering as a middle-aged troop commander. What he lacked in experience was compensated by a commonsense approach to the conduct of war and his high morale. The opponents of King Charles, whatever their political or economic motives, rallied to the cause of Puritanism. Cromwell fought for 'liberty of conscience' with the same unquestioning ardour which later generations of quite un-Puritan mercenary soldiers have bestowed on their regimental colours.

We know practically nothing of his work as a captain, except that he chose honest, God-fearing men. He was something of a pioneer of personnel selection, prepared to throw the net wide to get hard-fighting officers, whether of gentle birth or not. In one sense only was his choice of men narrow. He selected his followers entirely from the Independent sects, among 'the godly'. As we have seen, he went to considerable trouble to rid himself of Presbyterian officers during 1644 and 1645, and of political opponents, however close they had once been to him, at every stage on his journey. What other general in history ever sacked all the troop commanders of his own regiment as Oliver did in 1658?

There is no question that the crises of his career often found him hesitant, and this may have been part of his make-up from the first. Nevertheless, he usually succeeded in overcoming this weakness in the field. We have seen perhaps a trace of it at Grantham, but there he was not the overall commander. We have seen it, too, after the first charge at Marston Moor, but then he had been wounded and may have been temporarily off-balance.

The regimental histories of the First Civil War have attracted the attention of some historians, but as yet the picture is not as clear as one could wish. What were the crack units of those long vanished armies? Prince Rupert's regiment of horse, Newcastle's Whitecoats, Hesilrige's Lobsters: these all seem to have earned the title, to name only a few. There can be no question that Cromwell's famous double regiment of Ironsides was in the very forefront. Well-horsed, 'extraordinarily armed', sternly disciplined, their only military fault was their tendency—inevitable in a revolutionary army—to be too politically minded. It seems that they were repulsed at Second Newbury, but that can happen to anyone. It is possible that there have been units which never met with a reverse. If so, they probably saw but little service.

Gainsborough was Cromwell's great day as a regimental commander, and there he proved himself a cool hand. He was no *sabreur*. If he ever killed his man in some half-forgotten *mêlée*, history has not recorded it. He was no doubt a good horseman, but one does not imagine him cutting his way out of a tight corner as Rupert did at Newark and Marston Moor. He did not lack a certain *joie de combattre*, as was seen before Naseby and Dunbar, but it was the zealous enthusiasm of the crusader, the iconoclast, rather than the more straightforward love of a fight, characteristic of the Palatine Princes.

As a cavalry general Cromwell was no hothead. At Marston Moor he probably led the first charge of his wing, but at Naseby he came on at the head of the second line, to support the first wave and follow up their success by putting in his reserve where there was most need. At Dunbar he acted in similar fashion, rallying his troops before launching the pursuit. Both at Marston Moor and Naseby, Fairfax, a younger man and a fire-eater, led the last charge, and on the latter occasion at least he was, of course, senior to Cromwell. This is not to reflect upon Oliver's personal courage: his conduct was natural in a man of maturer years. It merely illustrates his method of going about things. He liked to see what was going on, and to influence the battle with his reserves. This may not have been the technique of Gustavus Adolphus or Pappenheim, but it was successful—and after all they had both got themselves killed. *En passant*, it is worth remarking that Cromwell had probably read fairly full details of their fate in *The Swedish Intelligencer* or some similar news-sheet. One feels that Wellington would have approved of Cromwell. The Duke was always complaining that British cavalry only knew how to gallop. Cromwell's chief virtue as a cavalry officer was his ability to keep something in hand and to rally his men when the impetus of their first charge was spent. His personal bravery was amply proved by his leadership at Drogheda, the passage of the Severn at Worcester, and by his single-handed charge against Lilburne's mutinous regiment.

Cromwell's experience in the First Civil War was mainly as a cavalry officer. He did take part in certain sieges, notably Basing House, meeting with no very severe problem, except at Faringdon Castle, where his attempt at escalade met with a rude repulse. It is very doubtful whether the attempt was worth risking, particularly in daylight, though Picton's Division at Badajoz, in an age when weapons were more efficient, succeeded under even worse conditions. In 1648 at Pembroke Castle, lacking heavy artillery, he again attempted an assault, but in vain, and he was reduced to starving the place into submission.

The war in Ireland was for Oliver entirely one of sieges. At Drogheda he went through the customary moves of seventeenth-century warfare: summons, breach, assault. He may have under-estimated the opposition, for only his personal intervention in the third assault won the day. It is an anxious business waiting for the success of the stormers. Perhaps the savagery of the slaughter which followed is partly accounted for by a loss of self-control following a fairly prolonged period of nervous strain. Of his other Irish sieges only Clonmel needs mention now. Here Oliver met with the most costly repulse of his whole career. One is left with the impression that Cromwell was not at his best in siege work. It is odd that a contemporary said of Rupert, who is generally regarded as the archtype of *beau sabreur*, that sieges were 'his masterpiece'. The fact is that Rupert was a professional soldier and that Cromwell was not. The minutiae of an art which, even before the days of Vauban and Coehorn, was complicated in the extreme, were not to be mastered by an officer who was picking up his new trade as he went along.

Cromwell commanded detached columns in the First Civil War, but he had no field army of his own until the Second. His reputation as a general must depend largely on his conduct of three campaigns, those of Preston, Dunbar and Worcester. At Preston and Dunbar he scored great tactical successes against severe odds. Hamilton was no general, but nevertheless Cromwell must be given great credit for the relentless pursuit which followed his success at Preston. At Dunbar we find him fighting his way out of a tight corner by good tactics and the sheer fighting quality of the army he had built up. His opponent, Leslie, was no mean general, and for that reason Oliver's victory is the more creditable. At the same time, nobody must expect praise for the strategy which brought him to Dunbar, with the Scots across his lines of communication. We must turn to the Worcester campaign to find the now aging general displaying his real quality as a strategist. To encourage the Scots to follow once more the route that Hamilton had taken in 1648 was a considerable risk, particularly from the political point of view. Had the Royalists scored some notable success, the result could have been fatal to Oliver's personal position. But indeed Cromwell's strategy was never sounder than in the campaign of 1651. If one may cite the somewhat hackneyed 'Principles of War', by fighting in England he was able to achieve Concentration of Force, and to throw his net around an enemy who awaited him like a host of hypnotized rabbits. The most remarkable feature of the battle that followed is, of course, the use of the bridges of boats. Surely this is evidence of a certain originality in the old Ironside's mind? It is not easy to find examples of the successful passage of a major river obstacle in the midst of a battle.

At this point most authors leave the problem of Cromwell as a soldier. But there was one more war for the conduct of which he was responsible: the Spanish war of 1655. This time it is true that he struck no stroke in person, but war is waged on at least four levels, two tactical and two strategic. We have seen Cromwell operating at the tactical levels. We have had evidence of his strategic work—at the Montgomery, Rommel level of Alamein days—from 1648 to 1651. Now he was to operate as Protector and Lord General, as National Leader—at the Winston Churchill level. The war with Spain was probably a mistake. Cromwell miscalculated, for he did not expect his West Indian adventure to lead to war. His hopes of gaining great wealth thereby were not fulfilled. Blake's exploits brought his government international repute, but little hard cash. At Dunkirk the redcoats won renown, but the seizure of Jamaica was the only lasting gain. The war proved an unwarrantable strain on the resources of Cromwell's government. It should not have been beyond the wit of man to see that this would be so. Nor should it have been too difficult for the Protector, with his 160 warships and his 47,000 troops, to have fitted out the expedition of Penn and Venables in a manner worthy of the New Model Army.

Much has been written of Cromwell as a soldier, most of it in terms of unbounded adulation. If I have ventured, while attempting

25 CROMWELL
Detail, enlarged about four times, from the unfinished miniature by Samuel Cooper

26 CROMWELLIAN GOLD 'BROAD'
(enlarged)

27 SECOND GREAT SEAL OF THE
PROTECTOR, 1655 (reduced)
Designed by Thomas Simon

to analyse his triumphs, to point to his failures, I have not done so in the spirit of that school of angry young commentators, who take pleasure in painting the heroes of other days as 'donkeys'. Quite the contrary. Yet uncritical hero-worship is not a useful approach to the military art. Ironsides was a stout-hearted soldier, who won his way to the front by personality, common sense, sheer hard fighting, and an innate talent for war. By 1646 he was the idol of the Army, which was to be the chief—indeed the only—pillar of his throne in the years to come.

★   ★   ★

'Peace hath her victories' . . . but they succeeded in eluding Cromwell.

A stout heart and a firm faith had sustained the Calvinist crusader on many a stricken field. The countless successes vouchsafed to the Lord's Anointed had been clear proof of the justice of the 'good old cause'. At Westminster and at Whitehall in the period after the First Civil War he was to find problems every bit as complicated as any he met in his eight campaigns. And he was to prove but ill-equipped by temperament, education and experience for his work as statesman and politician.

Temperamentally, his chief drawback in his political life was not the melancholy which had dogged his early years, nor the hesitation which so often preceded his big decisions: it was the passionate temper which even when he was over fifty would sometimes break out. He was well aware of this weakness and, on occasion, was known to apologize for it in a handsome manner, as he did to Lord Wharton: 'I was untoward when I spake last with you . . . I spake cross . . . I have known my folly do good when affection has overcome my reason'. A righteous rage is no bad thing in an army commander, and, since with Cromwell it blew over almost as quickly as it came, it never seems to have done him any harm as a soldier. But who can estimate the legacy of vengeful hatred that the dissolution of the Rump left to dog him through his last five years? Vane and the rest never forgave him. At the Restoration, when it came, Hesilrige went to the Tower and Scot to the scaffold, yet neither lost any opportunity to pull down the Protector who alone stood between them and destiny.

It may seem strange to assert that he was ill prepared by his political experience for high office. After all, he had been in Parliament as long ago as 1628; he had been in both Short and Long Parliaments, and he had also been a Justice of the Peace. Even so, he had not been one of the leaders of Pym's party; his political interests had been confined to religious and military affairs, and the fen drainage dispute of his East Anglian neighbours. How often did he have the opportunity to appear at Westminster between 1642 and 1646? He certainly made his mark in the debate over the Self-Denying Ordinance, but it seems he had little opportunity to take his seat during the war years. Those four years were indeed a complete break in his life. The intense activity of wartime soldiering left but little time for political speculation. Oliver had long looked for a field in which to give rein to his natural abilities. He did not find this in the sessions of the Long Parliament: it was in the wars that he was first compelled to extend himself.

His political record is marred by many blunders. Ignoring his choice of party in the great struggle of his day, what defence can there be for the execution of the King, for which his greatest admirers admit his responsibility? What real chance did it leave of any settlement with the Royalists? The massacre at Drogheda, however justifiable by the rules of war, did lasting harm, as did his Irish 'settlement'. His dealings with his Parliaments are a sorry story of misplaced confidence, and were founded on a series of miscalculations. In the field of domestic policy one can say much good of his religious toleration of 'the godly', which undoubtedly shielded the birth pangs of the Quaker movement, and permitted the return of the Jews to England. It did not include the Roman Catholics or the Anglicans, but even so, Cromwell was notably tolerant for his age and for his party.

As to the major-generals and the 'Decimation Tax', his staunchest supporter would be hard put to it to find any good to say of them. Of his foreign policy Pepys was to write: 'What brave things he did and made all the neighbour princes fear him'. In that field the Protector did well to end the Dutch War, but his policy of war with Spain and the alliance with France have been much condemned. Though he intervened to protect the Protestants of the Vaudois, it is doubtful if this did much good, and though he would like to have based his foreign policy on a League of Protestant powers, he was in fact compelled by circumstances, like most statesmen before or since, to follow a policy that was 'all sordid, commercial and diplomatic' (Hill).

Worst of all, at a time when the country was relatively prosperous, he managed to leave the government insolvent.

To say that he was out of his depth as a national leader is not to attack his moral character. He was forced at every stage of his difficult journey to experiment. He had no means of knowing what would work and what would not. Though his strength was entirely in the Army, he hoped against hope to make it more broadly based, to govern constitutionally. Perhaps he was naïve to hope for this: at least he was sincere. Many have thought him a hypocrite. 'He will weep, howl and repent, even while he doth smite you under the first rib', wrote one of 'Freeborn John' Lilburne's friends. It is the fate of those who couch their thoughts in Biblical language to be misunderstood. Even if 'Cromwell is the most quotable man in English history', his language was often woefully lacking in precision. But this does not make him the hypocrite painted by Clarendon—the 'brave bad man'. On the contrary his personal character was admirable: a loving son, a faithful husband, an indulgent father; he had little personal ambition of the worldly sort. If he was occasionally vindictive, as to Slingsby, and perhaps Packer, he normally listened to the dictates of a tender conscience, leaving a record to shame the grosser dictators of latter days.

Unable to evolve a political system better than the one he had destroyed, he was doomed to failure. Even so, Cromwell himself was indispensable while the Army was the chief power in the land. If his government was really only a sort of 'caretaker government' awaiting the return of a King, who was there better fitted than he to rule? Lambert? Hesilrige? Heaven forbid! Cromwell's positive qualities, and notably his Calvinism, fitted him well for his work as a soldier, but left him in the dark as a statesman.

His own words are his best epitaph: 'None climbs so high as he who knows not whither he is going'.

*   *   *

SELECT BIBLIOGRAPHY

W. C. ABBOTT: *Writings and Speeches of Oliver Cromwell.* 4 volumes 1937-47.

ANON: *Boscobel.* 1680. Useful for the Battle of Worcester. 1651

MAURICE ASHLEY: *The Greatness of Oliver Cromwell.* 1957.

D. BRUNTON and D. H. PENNINGTON: *Members of the Long Parliament.* 1950.

LT.-COLONEL A. H. BURNE, D.S.O.: *Battlefields of England.* 1950. For the Battle of Worcester.

LT.-COLONELS A. H. BURNE and P. YOUNG: *The Great Civil War. A Military History.* 1959.

EARL OF CLARENDON: *The History of the Rebellion and Civil War in England.* Ed. W. D. Macray. Oxford. 1888.

GODFREY DAVIES: *The Early Stuarts, 1603-1660.* 1937.

GODFREY DAVIES: *Bibliography of British History: Stuart Period, 1603-1714.* 1928.

C. H. FIRTH: *The Battle of Dunbar.* Transactions of the Royal Historical Society. New Series, vol. XIV. 1900.

C. H. FIRTH: *Oliver Cromwell.* Heroes of the Nations Series. 1900.

C. H. FIRTH: *Cromwell's Army.* 3rd Edition. 1921.

C. H. FIRTH and GODFREY DAVIES: *The Regimental History of Cromwell's Army.* 1940.

S. R. GARDINER: *History of the Great Civil War, 1642-9.* 2nd Edition. 1893.

PAUL H. HARDACRE: *The Royalists during the Puritan Revolution.* 1956.

CHRISTOPHER HILL: *Oliver Cromwell.* Historical Association Pamphlet. 1958.

MARY FREAR KEELER: *The Long Parliament, 1640-1641.* 1954.

EDMUND LUDLOW: *Memoirs of Edmund Ludlow.* Oxford. 1894. Edited by Sir C. H. Firth.

JOSHUA SPRIGGE, M.A.: *Anglia Rediviva: England's Recovery.* 1647.

G. M. TREVELYAN, O.M.: *England under the Stuarts.* 1904.

H. R. TREVOR-ROPER: 'Oliver Cromwell and His Parliaments' in *Essays Presented to Sir Lewis Namier.* 1956.

DAVID UNDERDOWN: *Royalist Conspiracy in England 1649-1660*. 1960.

SIR EDWARD WALKER: *Historical Discourses*. 1705.

C. V. WEDGWOOD: *The King's Peace*. 1955.

C. V. WEDGWOOD: *The King's War*. 1959.

A. H. WOOLRYCH: *Penruddock's Rising, 1655*. Historial Association Pamphlet. 1955.

INDEX

The numerals in **heavy type** refer to the figure numbers of illustrations

Adwalton Moor, Battle of, 44
'Agitators', 80, 81
Andover, action at, 66
Argyll, Marquis of, 89
Armiger, Captain, 52
Ashe, John, M.P., 130
Assheton, Colonel Ralph, 88
Astley, Sir Jacob, Royalist general, 69, 70, 76
Aston, Sir Arthur, Royalist governor of Drogheda, 93, 94
Axtell, Colonel, 92
Ayscoghe, Captain Edward, 45, 46

Bagot, Colonel Richard, 38
Baillie, Robert, 53, 56
Baillie, William, Scottish general, 89
Balfour, Lt.-General Sir William, 33, 36, 37, 60, 61
Barebone Parliament, 117, 119, 120
Basing House, Siege of, 73-4, 82, 139
Bedford, Earl of, 33
Berkeley, Sir John, 76, 82
Berry, Captain-Lieutenant James, 36, 40, 45
Bethell, Major Christopher, 71
Blake, Admiral Robert, 113, 127, 128, 140; **21**
Bletchington House, 67, 68
Bolingbroke Castle, 47, 48
Boteler, Major-General, 127
Bradshaw, John, 92, 121
Brentford, storming of, 38
Bridgwater, Somerset, storming of, 72

Bristol, Siege of, 72
Broghill, Lord, 95
'Brownists,' 52, 53
Burges, Lt.-Colonel Roger, 67
Burghley House, taken, 44
Byron, Sir John, 1st Lord, 36, 37, 54, 55, 89

Callander, Earl of, 87, 88
Cambridge, 14, 35, 41, 52; **4**
Cannon, Captain Henry, 67
Carnwath, Earl of, 70
Cavendish, Lt.-General Charles, 42, 44, 45
Chalgrove Field, action at, 44
Charles I, King, 17, 18, 19, 20, 22, 24, 25, 26, 27, 28, 29, 31, 36, 50, 70, 71, 78, 79, 80, 81-2, 83, 84, 89, 90, 98, 113, 135
  at Edgehill, 36
  at Naseby, 70
  Trial and execution, 90-2; **17**
Charles II, 98, 99, 105, 106, 108, 109, 110, 123, 125
  crowned at Scone, 104
Claypole, John, 77, 129
Cleveland, Earl of, 60, 109
Clonmel, Siege of, 94, 95, 96, 139
'Clubmen', 72
Colchester, Siege of, 86, 135
Cork, taken, 95
Crauford, Major-General Lawrence, 51, 52, 53, 54, 55, 58, 59, 61, 62
Cromwell, Bridget, 77; **13**
Cromwell, Captain, Royalist cousin of Oliver, 41

Cromwell, Elizabeth (Mrs. Clay-
pole), 77; **6**
death of, 135
Cromwell, Henry, 77, 96
Cromwell, Oliver, parentage, 13; **5**
education, 14
physique, 14–15, 32
character, 14–15, 23, 30, 77, 141
interests, 16
'Lord of the Fens', 18, 38, 141
Children, 32, 77; **6**
Captain, 32
Colonel, 38
in London, 77, 84; **16, 19**
Governor of Ely, 40, 47
Lt.-General, 49, 50
Lt.-General of New Model, 68
'Ironsides', 57, 68, 140
Lord Lieutenant of Ireland, 93
Protector, 14, 15, 16, 119, 131
Parliament, 17, 22, 23–4, 64, 115;
22
Death, 136; **23**
Portraits of, **1, 3, 25**
Cromwell, Oliver, eldest surviving
son, 35
death of, 52
Cromwell, Richard, 14, 77; **12**
Cromwell, Sir Oliver, 36
Cropredy Bridge, Action at, 58, 65
Crowland, Siege of, 41, 43

Dalbier, Colonel, 73–4
Dalziel, General Thomas, 108, 109
Deane, Richard, Admiral and
General, 108
Decimation Tax, 127, 129, 142
Dering, Sir Edward, M.P., 29–30
Desborough, Major John, 35, 36, 71,
131
Digby, Lord, 23, 29, 30
Drogheda, Storming of, 93, 95, 97,
138, 139, 142
Drury Lane, 77, 79
Dublin, 93
Dunbar, Battle of, 100–4, 106, 108,
134, 136, 138, 139, 140; **18, 20**
losses at, 103

Dunbar Medal (illus.), 105
Dunkirk, 132, 140
Dutch War, 113, 120, 121, 142

Eastern Association, 38, 43, 44, 49,
51, 52, 53, 57, 59, 60, 63, 65, 68
Edgehill, Battle of, 36, 38, 41, 93
Elector Palatine, 78
Eliot, Sir John, M.P., 17
Ely, 19, 32, 40, 41, 49, 68, 77
Essex, Earl of, Captain-General, 27,
33, 36, 37, 38, 39, 44, 58, 60, 63,
100
Ewer, Colonel, 86

Fairfaxes, 44
Fairfax, Lady, 92
Fairfax, Lord, 44, 52, 55
Fairfax, Sir Thomas, 44, 47, 48, 53,
54, 56, 57, 65, 66, 68, 70, 71, 72,
76, 78, 80, 81, 82, 83, 86, 89, 90,
91, 98, 108, 133, 138
Falkland, Lord, 27
Faringdon Castle, attempt on, 67,
139
Field Word, at Dunbar, *The Lord of
Hosts* (English), 102, 108; *The
Covenant* (Scots), 102
at Naseby, *God our Strength*
(Parliamentarian), 69; *Queen
Mary* (Royalist), 69
Fiennes, Captain John, 37
Fiennes, Nathaniel, 24;
portrait of, **10**
First Bishops' War, 20
Fleetwood, Charles, Parliamentarian
general, 78, 102, 108, 118, 131,
134
Fortescue, Major-General, 123
Fox, George, 135, 136

Gainsborough, 43, 44, 46, 47, 48, 50,
138
Gerard, John, 124
Glemham, Sir Thomas, Governor
of Oxford, 56, 75

Glencairn, William, Earl of, Rising in 1653, 110, 120, 121
Goffe, Colonel, 102
Goodwin, Vice-Admiral, 123
Goring, George, Royalist general, 54, 55, 56, 60, 62, 65, 66, 71, 72
Grand Remonstrance, 27, 28, 29, 30
Grantham, 42, 43, 48, 137
Grey, Lord, of Groby, 44
Guise, William, 107

Hamilton, Duke of, 86, 87, 88, 109, 139, 140
Hampden, John, 20, 22, 23, 27, 28, 29, 30, 31, 37, 38
  mortally wounded, 44
Harrison, Thomas, Major, later Parliamentarian general, 74, 88, 106, 109, 114, 115, 116, 117, 118, 134
Hastings, Henry, Royalist general, 38
Hereford, 72
Hesilrige, Sir Arthur, 15, 28, 87, 100, 104, 114, 121, 122, 132, 141, 143
Hewitt, Dr., 135
Hitch, Canon, of Ely, 49–50
Hodgson, Captain John, 86, 101, 103
Holland, War with, 113, 120, 121, 142
Holles, Denzil, M.P., 24, 27, 28, 37, 78, 81, 89
Hopton, Sir Ingram, 48
Hopton, Lord, 76
Horton, Colonel Thomas, 85, 86, 95
Hotham, Captain John, 44
Hotham, Sir John, 29, 42,
Huntingdon, 13, 14, 15, 17, 18, 35, 40
Huntingdonshire, 24, 29, 41
Hyde, Edward, later Earl of Clarendon, 24, 25, 30

Ingoldsby, Colonel Richard, 108
Ireland, Rebellion in, 26, 33, 93–7, 98

Ireton, Henry, 40, 69, 72, 77, 78, 79, 80, 81, 82, 90, 93, 95, 96, 98, 104, 117; 15
'Ironsides' (Cromwell), 57, 68, 140
Ironsides (Regt.), 62, 66, 95, 137
Islip, action at, 66

Jones, Colonel Michael, 93, 95
Joyce, Cornet George, 79

Keightlye, Captain, 37
Keith, Sir William, 108
Kimbolton, Lord, later Earl of Manchester, 53
Kineton, 36, 37

Lambert, Major-General, 81, 86, 89, 90, 99, 101, 102, 104, 105, 106, 109, 114, 117, 118, 119, 120, 121, 131, 134, 143; 11
Langdale, Sir Marmaduke, Royalist general, 68, 69, 86, 87, 88
Langford House, taken, 75
Langport, Battle of, 71
Laud, Archbishop, 14, 18, 20, 26
Laugharne, Major-General Rowland, 85
Lavington, action at, 66
Le Hunt, Captain Richard, 52 (fn.)
Leighton, Colonel Sir William, 135
Lenthall, William, Speaker of the House of Commons, 28, 59 116, 121
  despatches to, 105, 107, 109
Leslie, General David, 53, 55, 56, 57, 99, 100, 101, 104, 105, 106, 108, 139
Levellers, 83, 90, 119, 120, 121, 124
Leven, Earl of, 52, 54, 57
Lilburne, John, 19, 22, 23, 51, 78, 80, 83, 84, 107, 120, 138, 143; 8
Lincoln, 48, 50, 52
Lisle, Colonel George, 70
London Trained Bands, 38, 58
Londonderry, 95
Long, Colonel James, 66

Long Parliament, 30, 31, 97, 98, 111, 112, 121, 127, 133, 141, 142
Lostwithiel, 58
Lowestoft, 41
Lucas, Sir Charles, Royalist general, 55, 56
Ludlow, Lieutenant-General Edmund, 84, 112
Lynn, Siege of, 47

Maidstone, Cromwell's steward, 14
Maidstone, storming of, 86
Manchester, Earl of, 18, 24, 39, 47, 48, 49, 50, 51, 52, 53, 54, 55, 57, 58, 60, 61, 62, 63, 64. See also Kimbolton
Mandeville, Lord, 24, 25, 28
Mardyke, 132
Margery, Captain Ralph, 40
Marston Moor, Battle of, 53–7, 59, 99, 108, 125, 137, 138
Marten, Henry, 91, 92
Massey, Major-General Edward, 81, 106
Maurice, Prince, 69
Mazarin, Cardinal, 113, 120
Meldrum, Sir John, Parliamentarian general, 44, 45, 46, 52
Mercurius Pragmaticus, 98
Middleton, Lt.-General John, 61
Milton, John, 49, 111, 112
Monck, George, Parliamentarian general and admiral, 101, 102, 110, 121
Monson, Sir John, 127
Montague, Colonel Edward, 74
Montgomery, Scottish Major-General, 108
Montrose, Marquis of, 98, 99
Moody, Captain John, 52 (fn.)
Moody, Captain Samuel, 52 (fn.)
Munro, Major-General, 87, 89
Musgrave, Sir Philip, 86, 87

Naseby, 68, 79, 102, 134, 135, 138
Naylor, James, 129
Newark, 41, 42, 44, 48, 52, 138

Newbury, First battle of, 93
Newbury, Second battle of, 58, 59, 61, 62, 63, 65, 138
Newcastle, Marquis of, 44, 46, 47, 52, 53, 54, 56
Newcastle, Siege of, 57
New Model Army, 52, 64, 65–76, 78, 81, 82, 90, 91, 140
Nineteen Propositions, 31–2
Northampton, Earl of, 66
Norwood, Major Henry, 124

O'Neill, Hugh, Royalist general, 95
Ormonde, Earl of, 93, 97
Overton, Colonel, 102
Owen, Rev. John, 112
Oxford, 37, 66, 67, 76
Oxford Parliament, 50

Packer, Major William, 134, 143
Palgrave, Colonel Sir John, 44
Parliamentary Army, Cavalry—arms and uniform, 33; composition—tactics, 33
    Artillery, 34–5
    Infantry—arms and uniform, 34
Patterson, Captain (?) William, 52 (fn.)
Pell, Lt.-Colonel Sir Bartholomew, 75
Pembroke Castle, 86, 139
Penn, Admiral William, 122, 127, 140
Penruddock, Colonel John, 125, 126, 127
Pepys, Samuel, quoted, 142
Percy, Lord, taken, 66
Peterborough (city), 41
Peterborough, Earl of, 33
Petition of Rights, 17
Pickering, Colonel, 74
Pitscotty, Colonel Cullom, 108
Pontefract Castle, Siege of, 89
Powick Bridge, Action at, 36, 108
Poyer, Colonel John, 85, 86, 89
Preston, Battle of, 87, 88, 139
Pride, Colonel Thomas, 102, 135

'Pride's Purge', 90, 119, 121
Pym, John, 17, 22, 23, 24, 25, 26, 27, 28, 29, 30, 31, 35, 49, 142; **9**

Ramsay, Colonel Sir James, 36
Roundway Down, Battle of, 44
Rump, The, 111–16, 117, 119, 133, 141
Rupert, Prince, 33, 36, 37, 52, 53, 54, 55, 56, 57, 69, 70, 138, 139

St. Ives, Huntingdonshire, 18
St. John, Oliver, 20, 22, 30, 35, 49, 59
Scots Commissioners 63, 85, 98, 100, 102
Second Bishops' War, 21, 22
Self-Denying Ordinance, 64, 66, 68, 142
Ship Money, 20, 22, 23
Shrewsbury, 36, 52
Sidney, Algernon, M.P., 116
Sindercombe, Miles, 129
Skippon, Major-General Philip, 33, 60, 61, 62, 69, 79
Slingsby, Colonel Sir Henry, M.P., 135, 143
Solemn League and Covenant, 49
Southampton, Earl of, 127
Spain, War with, 128, 132, 140, 142
Stapleton, Colonel Sir Philip, M.P., 78
Star Chamber, Court of, 19, 23, 29
Stayner, Captain (naval) Sir Richard, 128, 129
Steward family, 13–14, 19
Strafford, Earl of, 97
Strode, William, M.P., 23, 28, 31
Swallow, Robert, 40
Sweden, Queen Christina of, 128
    King Charles Gustavus of, 128

Thornhagh, Colonel Francis, 88
Thurloe, John, 124, 125, 130, 132, 135
Tillier, Major-General Henry, Royalist, 54, 56

Trevor, Colonel Marcus, 55
Triennial Act, 23, 30
Turenne, 132

Urry, Major-General Sir John, 54

Vane, Sir Henry, 24, 30, 49, 100, 114, 115; **14**
Van Tromp, Admiral, 113
Venables, Colonel, 95, 123, 127, 140
Vermuyden, Colonel Cornelius, 48

Waller, Colonel Sir Hardress, 74
Waller, Sir William, Parliamentarian general, 44, 58, 60, 63, 65, 66, 74, 76
Walton, Captain, later Colonel, Valentine, 29, 35, 40, 56, 58
Warwick, 36, 37
Warwick, Sir Philip, 15–16, 18, 23, 26, 27, 30, 36
Waterford, besieged, 94, 95
Waterhouse, Major, 135
Wentworth, Lord, Royalist general, 76
Wentworth, Sir Peter, M.P., 115
West Indies, Expedition to, 122–3, 127, 128
Wexford, Siege of, 95, 96, 97
Whalley, Major, later Major-General, Edward, 40, 46, 51, 65, 69, 71, 102, 127
Wharton, Lord, 141
White, Captain, 44
White, Major, 102
Whitelocke, Bulstrode, 15, 38, 114, 128, 138
Widdrington, Sir William, 47, 48
Wilde, Major Thomas, 52 (fn.)
Wildman, John, 121
Williams, John, Archbishop of York, 50, 82
Williams, Richard, 13
Willoughby, Lord, of Parham, 42, 44, 46, 47, 50, 51
Wilmot, Henry, Royalist general, 36

Winchester, 73
Winchester, Marquis of, 73, 75
Windebank, Colonel Francis, 67
Wood, Lieutenant Thomas, 94
Worcester, 36, 136, 138, 139, 140

Wray, Sir Christopher, 50
Wyndham, Colonel, Governor of
    Bridgwater, 72

York, 52, 53, 56, 99